I0447937

FIRST YEAR REPORT

FINANCIAL FRAUD ENFORCEMENT TASK FORCE

2010

Members of the Financial Fraud Enforcement Task Force[1]

Department of Justice
   Criminal Division
   Civil Division
   Tax Division
   Antitrust Division
   Civil Rights Division
   United States Bankruptcy Trustees
   United States Attorneys' Offices
   Federal Bureau of Investigation
   United States Marshals Service
Securities and Exchange Commission
Commodity Futures Trading Commission
Federal Trade Commission
Internal Revenue Service,
   Criminal Investigation Division
United States Postal Inspection Service
United States Secret Service
United States Immigration and
   Customs Enforcement
Department of the Treasury
Office of Thrift Supervision
Office of the Comptroller of the Currency
Financial Crimes Enforcement Network
Department of Commerce
Department of Labor
Department of Housing and
   Urban Development
Department of Education

Department of Homeland Security
Federal Deposit Insurance Corporation
Board of Governors of the Federal
   Reserve System
Federal Housing Finance Agency
Small Business Administration
Social Security Administration
Recovery Accountability and
   Transparency Board
National Credit Union Administration
North American Securities Administrators
   Association
Special Inspector General for the
   Troubled Asset Relief Program
Offices of Inspectors General, including:
   Department of Justice
   Department of the Treasury
   Department of Housing and
      Urban Development
   Department of Homeland Security
   U.S. Postal Service
   General Services Administration
   Small Business Administration
   National Science Foundation
   Federal Housing Finance Agency
National Association of Attorneys General
National District Attorneys Association

[1]Additional members have joined the Task Force within the past year.

Table of Contents

Introduction by Attorney General Eric H. Holder Jr., Chairman of the Financial Fraud Enforcement Task Force

Introduction

Eric H. Holder Jr.
Attorney General
Chairman, Financial Fraud
Enforcement Task Force

The financial crisis has impacted every American. It has presented not only fraud and deception in the finance and housing markets that helped fuel the crisis, but also the potential for fraudulent schemes to misuse the public's unprecedented investment in economic recovery. While we are aggressively confronting fraud born of the financial crisis, the reality is that we cannot prosecute our way out of the situation. Instead, we must address it with an equally broad and comprehensive enforcement response. This is the mission of the Financial Fraud Enforcement Task Force.

The Financial Fraud Enforcement Task Force was created by President Obama in November 2009 as the largest coalition ever brought to bear to confront fraud. Its membership is broad, consisting of several Department of Justice components, the Department of the Treasury, the Department of Housing and Urban Development, the Depart-

ment of Commerce, the Department of Labor, the Department of Homeland Security, the Securities and Exchange Commission, the Commodity Futures Trading Commission, the Federal Deposit Insurance Corporation, the Federal Home Finance Agency, the Financial Crimes Enforcement Network, the Federal Reserve Board, the Federal Trade Commission, the Internal Revenue Service — Criminal Investigation, the Office of the Comptroller of the Currency, the Office of Thrift Supervision, the Recovery Accountability and Transparency Board, the Special Inspector General for the Troubled Asset Relief Program, the U.S. Postal Inspection Service, the U.S. Secret Service, federal inspectors general, state attorneys general and many others. The President's Executive Order directs the Task Force to focus on the full array of corrupt conduct presented by the financial crisis, including securities and commodities fraud, bank fraud, mail and wire fraud, mortgage fraud, money laundering, False Claims Act violations, discrimination, and other financial crimes and violations. This far-reaching list, however, only begins to capture the breadth — and depth — of this massive interagency effort.

As the President set forth in his Executive Order, the Task Force has a clear mandate — to use the full criminal and civil enforcement resources of the federal government, along with state and local partners, to pursue a five-part mission:

- to investigate and prosecute financial crimes and other violations relating to the current financial crisis and economic recovery efforts;

- to recover the proceeds for such crimes and violations;

- to address discrimination in the lending and financial markets;

◆ to enhance coordination and cooperation among federal, state and local authorities responsible for the investigation and prosecution of financial crimes and violations; and

◆ to conduct outreach to the public, victims, financial institutions, nonprofit organizations, state and local governments and agencies, and other interested partners to enhance detection and prevention of financial fraud schemes.

To make this mission a reality, we designed the Task Force to prioritize the types of financial fraud that affect us most during this time of economic recovery: mortgage fraud, securities and commodities fraud, financial discrimination, and potential frauds preying upon the response to the economic crisis, including the funds disbursed through the American Recovery and Reinvestment Act and the Troubled Asset Relief Program. We established working groups to focus on these priority areas, bringing together top subject-matter experts from agencies at an operational level to work together. Whether it is case referrals, information sharing, case coordination or public outreach, we are far more effective and efficient when we combine our efforts.

I am pleased to report that the Task Force has responded to its broad mandate with impressive results. As more fully detailed in this report, the Task Force has made great strides in its inaugural year:

The Task Force is facilitating increased investigation and prosecution of financial crimes and other violations relating to the current financial crisis and economic recovery efforts, as well as the recovery of the proceeds for such crimes and violations. As explained in this annual report, there have been impressive criminal, civil and regulatory enforcement efforts by the many Task Force members in 2010, with thousands of enforcement actions addressing a broad array of fraud. For example, during one week in June 2010 alone, the Task Force members announced the indictment of the orchestrator of a multi-billion dollar complex fraud scheme that contributed to the failure one of the nation's largest banks, as well as the largest mortgage fraud sweep in history.

The Task Force is enhancing coordination and cooperation among federal, state and local authorities responsible for the investigation and prosecution of financial crimes and violations. We have developed a comprehensive enforcement network by establishing Financial Fraud Coordinators in every U.S. Attorney's Office in the country to coordinate Task Force efforts at the line level. We have strengthened and expanded that network by incorporating existing national and regional financial fraud task forces and increasing the number of collaborative anti-fraud efforts at the local level, such as the 94 regional mortgage fraud working groups and task forces around the country. We have armed that network with more tools and better trained personnel by compiling and distributing a resource guide of financial databases across enforcement agencies, holding national training conferences spanning the broad range of financial fraud areas, launching a website with fraud reporting and public education resources drawn from the full complement of government agencies, and tracking and distributing information about emerging fraud trends.

The Task Force is addressing discrimination in the lending and financial markets. During the first year of the Task Force, the Department of Justice received more referrals from the Department of Housing and Urban Development and others for potential discriminatory conduct than at any time in at least 20 years. The Task Force expects that these referrals, and other enforcement actions taken by the

Task Force members, will yield an increased number of cases in 2011. This would be in addition to the millions of dollars that Task Force members recovered for victims of discrimination through enforcement actions brought in 2010.

The Task Force is conducting outreach to the public, victims, financial institutions, nonprofit organizations, state and local governments and agencies, and other interested partners to enhance detection and prevention of financial fraud schemes. Understanding that our most powerful tool in combating financial fraud is an informed public, the Task Force has engaged in training and outreach efforts spanning every type of financial fraud and reaching every level of consumer, including government officials, business professionals and private citizens. In the Recovery Act area alone, the Task Force conducted one of the largest anti-fraud training efforts in history in order to help safeguard Recovery Act funds from fraud, waste and abuse. The Task Force has prioritized victim assistance and launched a website that serves as a "one-stop-shop" for the public to report fraud and to obtain information on how to avoid becoming victims.

While we have accomplished much in the first year of the Task Force, our work is far from complete. A healthy economy and, in these times, a full economic recovery, requires our continued vigilance in protecting American businesses and consumers from financial fraud. This Task Force has risen to the challenge and is prepared for the still difficult road ahead. I look forward to reporting on our continued success.

Overview of the
First Year of the Task Force

Overview

Robb Adkins
Executive Director
Financial Fraud Enforcement Task Force
Department of Justice, Office of the
Deputy Attorney General

In November 2009, the President created the Financial Fraud Enforcement Task Force by Executive Order. (See Appendix A). Composed of more than 25 federal agencies, regulators and inspectors general, as well as state and local partners, it is the largest coalition ever brought to bear in confronting fraud. And as the Executive Order directs, the Task Force is charged with addressing an exceptionally wide array of fraudulent activities: "bank, mortgage, and lending fraud; securities and commodities fraud; retirement plan fraud; mail and wire fraud; tax crimes; money laundering; False Claims Act violations; unfair competition; discrimination; and other financial crimes and violations."

The Executive Order directs the Task Force to use the full criminal and civil enforcement resources of the member departments and agencies: (1) to investigate and prosecute financial crimes and other violations relating to the current financial crisis and economic recovery efforts; (2) to recover the proceeds for such crimes and violations; (3) to address discrimination in the lending and financial markets; (4) to enhance coordination and cooperation among federal, state and local authorities responsible for the investigation and prosecution of financial crimes and violations; and (5) to conduct outreach to the public, victims, financial institutions, non-profit organizations, state and local governments and agencies, and other interested partners to enhance detection and prevention of financial fraud schemes.

The Executive Order's directives are reflected in the organization of the Task Force. We have established working groups composed of the subject-matter experts in each priority area:

♦ **The Training and Information Sharing Committee**, co-chaired by H. Marshall Jarrett, Director of the Executive Office for U.S. Attorneys (EOUSA) of the Justice Department; and James H. Freis Jr., Director of the Financial Crimes Enforcement Network (FinCEN).

♦ **The Enforcement Committee**

> *The Mortgage Fraud Working Group*, co-chaired by Tony West, Assistant Attorney General for the Civil Division of the Justice Department; Benjamin Wagner, U.S. Attorney for the Eastern District of California; Sharon Ormsby, Chief, Financial Crimes Section of the Federal Bureau of Investigation; Michael P. Stephens, Acting Inspector General of the Department of Housing and Urban Development-Office of Inspector General; and the National Association of Attorneys General, represented by Attorneys General Tom Miller of Iowa and Rob McKenna of Washington.

> *The Recovery Act Fraud Working Group*, co-chaired by Christine Varney, Assistant Attorney General for the Antitrust Division of the Justice Department; Lanny Breuer, Assistant Attorney General for the Criminal Division of the Justice Department; and Earl Devaney, Chairman of the Recovery Accountability and Transparency Board.

> *The Rescue Fraud Working Group*, co-chaired by Christy Romero, Acting Special Inspector General for the Troubled Asset Relief Program; Christian Weideman,

Chief Counsel for the Office of Financial Stability of the Treasury Department; and Lanny Breuer, Assistant Attorney General for the Criminal Division of the Justice Department.

The Securities and Commodities Fraud Working Group, co-chaired by Lanny Breuer, Assistant Attorney General for the Criminal Division of the Justice Department; Preet Bharara, U.S. Attorney for the Southern District of New York; Robert Khuzami, Director of Enforcement for the Securities and Exchange Commission (SEC); and David Meister, Director of Enforcement for the Commodity Futures Trading Commission.

The Non-Discrimination Working Group, co-chaired by Thomas Perez, Assistant Attorney General for the Civil Rights Division of the Justice Department; Michelle Aronowitz, Deputy General Counsel for Enforcement and Fair Housing of the Department of Housing and Urban Development (HUD); Sandy Braunstein, Director of the Division of Consumer and Community Affairs of the Federal Reserve Board; and the National Association of Attorneys General, represented by Attorney General Lisa Madigan of Illinois.

◆ **The Victims' Rights Committee**, co-chaired by EOUSA Director H. Marshall Jarrett and Mary Lou Leary, Principal Deputy Assistant Attorney General for the Office of Justice Programs (OJP) of the Justice Department.

Through the Task Force, we have put in place a structure that draws from the collective wisdom and expertise of the many member agencies but is still nimble enough to adapt to emerging schemes, capture lessons learned from one context and apply them to others, and share information and training.

To further these goals, every U.S. Attorney's Office has established a Financial Fraud Coordinator to ensure that aggressive fraud enforcement at the line level is pursued in all corners of the country. The Financial Fraud Coordinators convened a national conference in mid-October in South Carolina, at which the participants discussed Task Force priorities and how to assist line prosecutors and other partners facilitate more effective fraud enforcement nationwide.

In a further effort to translate enforcement goals to a reality at the operational level, U.S. Attorneys' Offices are participating in a growing number of collaborative regional anti-fraud efforts, such as the 94 regional mortgage fraud working groups and task forces around the country, and regional financial fraud task forces in Virginia, Connecticut, Florida and elsewhere. Going forward, we expect the formation and utilization of regional efforts, which combine federal, state and local law enforcement officers and regulators, to continue to be effective.

The financial crisis is incredibly broad and the types of fraud that contribute to and prey upon the crisis are equally broad — including securities and commodities fraud, investment scams, mortgage foreclosure schemes, and efforts to defraud economic recovery programs. The Task Force was set up to address this wide array of fraud, and it has been effective in doing so. The committees and working groups of the Task Force — the enforcement experts — have produced impressive results in their first year.

IMPROVED TRAINING, INFORMATION SHARING AND COLLABORATION

The Training and Information Sharing Committee has been active in its first year of supporting Task Force members and their enforcement priorities. In addition to organizing the National Conference of Financial Fraud Coordinators, the committee has helped conduct numerous training courses at the National Advocacy Center in South Carolina, covering a variety of fraud subjects.

During its first year, all 14 committee members gave presentations to the full committee regarding their financial fraud datasets. Based on these in-depth presentations, the committee developed and distributed across the law enforcement and regulatory agency communities the *Resource Guide for Financial Investigations*, which currently includes descriptions of 22 data sources from 12 Task Force member agencies that are critical to the investigation and prosecution of financial fraud matters. The *Resource Guide* will be a valuable tool to assist in conducting financial fraud investigations and prosecutions, and the committee expects that it will expand the guide to include additional datasets in the future.

MORTGAGE FRAUD

The Mortgage Fraud Working Group is tasked with combating a wide range of fraud in the mortgage, finance and housing markets, including loan modification schemes, foreclosure rescue scams, loan origination fraud, reverse mortgage schemes, short sale frauds and builder bailout schemes. Mortgage fraud trends show that the fraud evolves with the cycles of the housing market and varies by geographic region. Accordingly, the working group has focused its efforts in different, hard-hit regions throughout the country.

The working group has held regional summits around the country in Miami, Detroit, Phoenix, Columbus, Fresno, and Los Angeles. In each location, the public came together to hear from law enforcement, victims, housing counselors, industry experts and others to assess the mortgage fraud issues in that community. The regional summits also included a closed session with regional law enforcement authorities, including the regional mortgage fraud working groups

and task forces, to discuss strategies, resources and initiatives to successfully combat mortgage fraud.

Increased efforts to combat mortgage fraud have seen dramatic enforcement results. In the first year of the Task Force, the number of mortgage fraud defendants charged by U.S. Attorneys' Offices has more than doubled from 526 in fiscal year 2009, to 1,235 in fiscal year 2010. There was a similar increase in the number of mortgage fraud cases charged, going from 267 in fiscal year 2009 to 656 in fiscal year 2010. And the emphasis on firm sentences for mortgage fraud followed the same trend for 2010, with a near doubling of the number of defendants sentenced to more than two, three and five years in prison. This increase has coincided with a near doubling of the number of regional mortgage fraud working groups and task forces nationwide.

The Mortgage Fraud Working Group helped increase not just the cases charged and sentences imposed for mortgage fraud, but also expanded the tools and strategies used to confront mortgage fraud. For example, from March 1, 2010, to June 17, 2010, the group spearheaded Operation Stolen Dreams, the largest mortgage fraud sweep in history. The mortgage fraud sweep was different from prior efforts not just in terms of its size, but also because it included a broad array of enforcement actions. The operation included charges, convictions and sentencings against a total of more than 1,500 criminal defendants. Civil enforcement actions were part of the sweep as well, with approximately 400 civil fraud defendants involved and nearly $200 million in civil recoveries ordered. And the sweep included not just federal prosecutions by U.S. Attorneys' Offices, but important participation by federal agencies such as the Federal Trade Commission (FTC), state attorneys general and district attorneys, and the use of bankruptcy actions and other enforcement means to confront fraud. These efforts reinforce the strength of the Task Force's strategy of bringing broad coalitions to bear and using all of the enforcement tools available to us. We expect this approach to continue to be effective.

RECOVERY ACT, PROCUREMENT AND GRANT FRAUD

According to the Recovery Board, by the close of 2010 the federal government had released approximately $600 billion in funds under the Recovery Act. Notwithstanding the substantial volume of funds now distributed, the number of prosecutions for Recovery Act-related offenses has been relatively low.

The lack of widespread fraud to date is due in significant part to the continuing efforts of the Recovery Board and the inspectors general, bolstered by the working group, to prevent fraud from happening in the first place, through such mechanisms as the Recovery Operations Center (ROC). The establishment of the Recovery Act, Procurement and Grant Fraud Working Group added the full weight of the law enforcement community behind the Recovery Board's efforts.

Because it was established at a stage when stimulus funds had yet to be distributed in significant quantities, the working group focused its early efforts on fraud prevention. Perhaps the most influential work done by the working group to date is the group's fraud prevention and detection training effort. At the close of 2010, more than 100,000 professionals responsible for awarding and overseeing Recovery Act funds, including inspectors, agents and prosecutors, were trained as part of this effort, and these numbers are only continuing to grow. This targeted fraud prevention and detection effort is one of the largest in history.

These efforts were punctuated by a flagship training event for agents, auditors and procurement and grant officers, entitled "Focus on Recovery," which was held on November 15-17, 2010, in Philadelphia. The Conference included speakers from the highest levels of the Justice Department and inspectors general community, as well as elected officials, including the Vice President of the United States. The conference was a tremendous success, attracting well over 500 attendees.

As we enter 2011, a critical foundation for the working group is the enforcement framework previously established by the National Procurement Fraud Task Force (NPFTF), which has now been merged into the working group, bringing together the community of inspectors general with the institutional knowledge of how to prevent and investigate procurement and grant fraud. The expertise that these inspectors general bring to the table will be of tremendous benefit for the working group as it moves forward in the year ahead.

TARP-RELATED FRAUD ENFORCEMENT

The Rescue Fraud Working Group is focused on the detection of fraud, waste and abuse, and increasing the robust and aggressive prosecution of crimes related to the Troubled Asset Relief Program (TARP). The working group has labored collectively to improve coordination and information sharing among agencies addressing rescue fraud, to enhance civil and criminal enforcement efforts, and to increase training and outreach opportunities for member agencies.

The working group made great progress in achieving these goals, including partnering throughout the country with working group members as well as state and local agencies to conduct investigations and to engage in outreach activities to familiarize authorities with SIGTARP resources and working group priorities.

The working group's efforts have translated to significant results within its first year. For example, on June 15, 2010, the Justice Department's Criminal Division and the U.S. Attorney's Office in the Eastern District of Virginia, working in partnership with SIGTARP and other Task Force members, charged Lee Bentley Farkas, former chairman of Taylor, Bean & Whitaker (TBW), for his role in a more than $2.9 billion fraud scheme that contributed to the failures of Colonial Bank and TBW. The scheme involved, among other things, an attempt to steal $553 million from TARP. Farkas was convicted on all counts in April 2011.

In another significant rescue fraud enforcement milestone, on October 8, 2010, Charles Antonucci, the former president and CEO of Park Avenue Bank, pleaded guilty in U.S. District Court for the Southern District of New York to securities fraud, making false statements to bank regulators, bank bribery and embezzlement of bank funds. Antonucci attempted to steal $11 million of TARP funds by, among other things, making fraudulent claims about the bank's capital position. With his guilty plea, Antonucci became the first defendant convicted of attempting to steal from the taxpayers' investment in TARP.

In the year ahead, the working group intends to continue to engage in collaborative enforcement efforts and outreach, with the goal of continuing to protect TARP funds from fraud, waste and abuse.

SECURITIES, COMMODITIES AND INVESTMENT FRAUD

The Securities and Commodities Fraud Working Group (SCFWG) brings together an impressive array of subject-matter experts in the enforcement of securities, commodities, corporate and investment frauds. Although many members of the SCFWG have a long history of collaboration, through the working group they have formed new initiatives, information-sharing efforts and training programs.

In the first year, SCFWG members conducted workshops on and discussed a number of important issues related to securities and commodities fraud enforcement, including the Dodd-Frank Wall Street Reform and Consumer Protection Act, the investigation and prosecution of investment fraud schemes, parallel criminal and civil proceedings, and the use of SEC administrative proceedings.

Apart from the formal meetings of the working group, SCFWG representatives communicate regularly to coordinate on specific investigations and prosecutions, as well as relevant policies. SCFWG members also participate in regional and state cooperative efforts, such as the Virginia Financial and Securities Fraud Task Force; the Connecticut Securities, Commodities and Investor Fraud Task Force; and the South Florida Securities and Investment Fraud Initiative.

The SCFWG members also have been active in public awareness and education. For example, to help people affected by the economic downturn, the FTC created ftc.gov/moneymatters, a website with information about avoiding scams, managing money and dealing with debt. As part of the Delivering Trust Campaign, the U.S. Postal Inspection Service developed a fraud prevention brochure with additional fraud prevention and awareness tips and mailed it to every household in the United States.

During 2010, SCFWG members investigated and prosecuted numerous significant securities, commodities and other investment frauds. The following are just a few of the many impressive enforcement results in 2010:

* As discussed above, in June 2010, the Criminal Division and the U.S. Attorney's Office for the Eastern District of Virginia, in partnership with other Task Force members, charged Lee Bentley Farkas with, among other things, securities fraud in connection with his role in a more than $2.9 billion fraud scheme that contributed to the failures of one of the 25 largest banks in the United States and one of the largest privately held mortgage lending companies. Subsequently, Farkas was convicted by a jury on all counts.

* In April 2010, the SEC filed charges against Goldman Sachs & Co. and one of its employees, Fabrice Tourre, alleging fraud in connection with the marketing of a synthetic collateralized debt obligation (CDO). On July 20, 2010, the court entered a consent judgment in which Goldman agreed to pay $550 million to settle the charges. The SEC's litigation continues against Fabrice Tourre.

* On April 8, 2010, Thomas J. Petters was sentenced to 50 years in prison, one of the longest financial crimes-related sentences in history, for engaging in $3.4 billion investment fraud that harmed hundreds of investors. In addition, lengthy prison terms were secured against Petters' co-conspirators. This case was the largest fraud case ever prosecuted in the District of Minnesota. Members of the SCFWG continue to investigate other individuals and companies related to the investment scheme.

* The CFTC filed 57 enforcement actions in Fiscal Year (FY) 2010, representing a 14 percent increase over the number of cases filed in FY 2009. During this period, the CFTC obtained judgments ordering the payment of more than $200 million in civil monetary penalties, restitution and disgorgement. During FY 2010, the number of investigations opened by the CFTC increased 66 percent from the prior fiscal year.

* On December 22, 2010, the FTC filed suit against 10 individuals and 61 corporations allegedly responsible for an Internet scheme that caused consumers to lose more than $275 million. The scheme lured consumers with allegedly false promises of government grants or money-making programs and, at its height, ensnared 15,000 consumers per day.

* In mid-December 2010, members of the SCFWG engaged in Operation Broken Trust, a nationwide three-and-a-half month effort to focus on direct-to-investor investment frauds, exposing the widespread prevalence of such schemes. The operation involved fraud schemes that harmed more than 120,000 victims throughout the country and caused more than $8 billion in losses.

Efforts to Combat Discrimination in the Housing and Finance Markets

The Task Force's Non-Discrimination Working Group focuses on financial fraud and other unfair practices directed at people or neighborhoods based on race, color, religion, national origin, sex, age, disability or any other basis prohibited by law. These practices take many forms, including charging minorities higher prices for credit, providing less favorable financial services to minority neighborhoods and steering minorities to more expensive loan products.

Throughout 2010, the members of the working group came together to discuss enforcement issues, to consider potential improvements through rulemaking and to sponsor outreach events for the public, enforcement authorities, housing counselors and industry representatives.

Again, increased collaboration has helped improve enforcement. In the first year of the Non-Discrimination Working Group, there was an increase in enforcement and in the number of investigations. In 2010, the bank regulatory agencies and HUD referred more matters involving a potential pattern or practice of discrimination to the Department of Justice than at any time in at least the last 20 years. The bank regulators and HUD combined referred 26 matters to the Department of Justice involving possible discrimination on the basis of race or national origin, which is more than twice as many as in the previous year.

Beyond increased information sharing and referrals, the working group members have also pursued significant enforcement actions. For example, in March 2010, the United States filed a fair lending complaint and consent order resolving *United States v. AIG Federal Savings Bank and Wilmington Finance Inc.*, in which two subsidiaries of AIG agreed to pay more than $6 million to resolve allegations that they engaged in a pattern or practice of discrimination against African American borrowers, and agreed to invest at least $1 million in consumer financial education.

UPHOLDING THE RIGHTS OF VICTIMS

Last, but certainly not least, is the Task Force's Victims' Rights Committee (VRC). The VRC's primary purpose is to address the needs and rights of victims of financial fraud. Accordingly, the committee has concentrated its efforts in three areas: (1) public awareness and education through the launch of a public website; (2) training on victims' rights and services; and (3) focusing on restitution as a priority in federal prosecutions.

During its first year, the VRC has worked to meet its goals by developing website content, training materials and legislative improvements aimed at addressing the needs and rights of financial fraud victims. The committee took the lead in establishing the Task Force's public website, *www.stopfraud.gov*, which was launched at a ceremony commemorating National Crime Victims' Rights Week. The website is an invaluable resource for members of the public, and contains descriptions of a wide variety of financial scams and information on how best to avoid becoming a victim of financial fraud. Beyond establishing the website, the VRC has also conducted numerous training sessions at national training events, and is currently working to develop an exportable training module that can be used by investigators, prosecutors and victim service providers to improve their awareness of and response to financial fraud victims.

Please visit *www.StopFraud.gov* to follow future fraud enforcement efforts around the country, obtain information on how the public can protect themselves from and report fraud, or to learn more about the Task Force. The following section of this report highlights some of the significant enforcement, outreach, training and initiatives of the Task Force members in 2010.

Task Force Member Contributions

TASK FORCE MEMBER CONTRIBUTIONS

TRAINING AND INFORMATION SHARING COMMITTEE

INTRODUCTION

The Training and Information Sharing Committee (TISC) is co-chaired by the Department of Justice (DOJ), Executive Office for U.S. Attorneys (EOUSA), represented by Director H. Marshall Jarrett and the Financial Crimes Enforcement Network (FinCEN), represented by Director James H. Freis Jr. The membership of the TISC consists of numerous federal organizations and agencies including the DOJ's Criminal, Civil, Antitrust and Civil Rights Divisions; the Attorney General's Advisory Committee; the Commodity Futures Trading Commission (CFTC); the U.S. Trustee Program; the FBI; the Internal Revenue Service-Criminal Investigation (IRS-CI); DOJ's Office of Justice Programs (OJP); the Recovery Accountability and Transparency Board (RATB); the Securities and Exchange Commission (SEC); and the Office of the Special Inspector General for the Troubled Asset Relief Program (SIGTARP). The primary purpose of the TISC is to formulate policy and to support the various Enforcement Committee Working Groups of the Task Force in the areas of training and information sharing.

OUTREACH AND INITIATIVES

To date the TISC has met a total of six times and each meeting has consisted of participating agencies briefing the committee members regarding the data sets they maintain and utilize to perform their law enforcement or regulatory functions. The meetings also involved in-depth discussions dedicated to exploring training opportunities that will best leverage the substantial resources of the broad Task Force membership. During its first year, the TISC heard briefings from all 14 committee members regarding their datasets. These presentations generally included a description of the type of information stored in the pertinent databases, how that information is used as part of the agency's mission and the means by which outside agencies can obtain access.

In addition to learning about the different databases utilized by committee members, the TISC also heard from member agencies who maintain resources dedicated to the tactical analysis of financial database information. These presentations included information on the FBI's Financial Intelligence Center, the Recovery Accountability and Transparency Board's sophisticated financial tracking and fraud detection database at the Recovery Operations Center as well as information from DOJ's Deputy Director for the National Information Exchange Model regarding the information sharing tool N-DEX and OneDOJ. Based on these in-depth presentations from the committee members regarding their most useful databases, the committee decided to develop and distribute across the law enforcement and regulatory agency communities a publication that identifies and describes the financial fraud data sets managed by Task Force member agencies that are critical to the investigation and prosecution of financial fraud. In the fall of 2010, the TISC completed the *Resource Guide for Financial Investigations*, which currently includes descriptions of 22 data sources from 12 agencies and was first disseminated at the Financial Fraud Coordinators' Conference in October 2010. The committee believes that the *Resource Guide* will be a valuable tool to assist members of the Task Force in conducting financial fraud investigations and prosecutions, and intends to further develop and refine the *Resource Guide* over time as new databases are developed and as additional entities join the Task Force.

The TISC has also been exploring various on-going information sharing efforts undertaken by agencies and entities outside of the committee. Among other presentations, the TISC has been briefed by: the Institute for Intergovernmental Research regarding Regional Information Systems Sharing (RISS); the Federal Trade Commission (FTC) regarding Consumer Sentinel; the Conference of State Banking Supervisors regarding the financial information they maintain and utilize; and the National White Collar Crime Center concerning their most recent statistics compiled on financial fraud. The TISC co-chairs also met with the Office of Management and Budget, Chief Information Officer, and his former Chief of Architecture, to learn about their efforts to gather information on various ongoing data sharing projects across federal, state and local governments. The TISC will continue to review the various information sharing efforts taking place across the government to ensure that Task Force members are aware of what valuable data sources are available in the fight against financial fraud and to identify potential redundancies that may be addressed in the future.

TRAINING AND COORDINATION

As conducting training is one of TISC's core missions, it is not surprising that the bulk of the Committee's efforts were focused in this area during the Task Force's first year. From conducting national training courses to collaborating with agencies within and outside of the Task Force, the TISC had many accomplishments in the area of training and coordination in 2010, including:

- *Nationwide Training Conferences:* As one of the Co-Chairs of the TISC, EOUSA conducts a significant amount of training for both attorneys and agents at the National Advocacy Center (NAC) in Columbia, South Carolina. During calendar year 2010, EOUSA organized the Mortgage Fraud Task Force Conference on

March 2-4, 2010, which brought together both state and federal prosecutors from each of the 75 regional state/federal mortgage fraud task forces and working groups in which U.S. Attorneys' Offices (USAOs) participated at that time. The purpose of the Conference was to allow the regional task forces to share and refine best practices and to learn from one another's challenges and successes. A general mortgage fraud seminar was held at the NAC in May 2010, and the White Collar Crime Seminar took place in July 2010. The TISC also helped organize the October 2010 Financial Fraud Coordinators' (FFC) Conference at the NAC, which was attended by the FFCs from nearly every district in the country.

- *Pursuing Additional Training Opportunities With Task Force Partners:* The TISC, in coordination with EOUSA's Office of Legal Education, also made a number of requests for additional financial fraud courses at the NAC for prosecutors and investigators for fiscal year 2011. Those requested courses included mortgage fraud, bank and securities fraud, mortgage fraud for auditors, bankruptcy fraud and others. The TISC has also been in contact with the Federal Law Enforcement Training Center (FLETC) to determine how best to partner with other Task Force members to prepare financial fraud training materials that can be used to train auditors and agents from around the country. Further, the TISC has initiated efforts to gather existing mortgage fraud training materials from the USAOs and law enforcement agencies in order to create a consolidated single training resource that can be easily disseminated to prosecutors and agents throughout the nation.

- *Use of Multi-Media To Enhance Training:* In addition to offering courses at the NAC, EOUSA operates the Justice Television Network, which provides training opportunities for Assistant U.S. Attorneys via the internet. In

November 2009, a fraud training program called, "Mortgage Fraud Basics," was made available on JTN. An additional video production, "Mortgage Fraud Rescue Schemes," will follow in calendar year 2011.

◆ *National Outreach to Line Prosecutors:* The TISC assisted in the gathering and editing of articles for the September 2010 issue of the *United States Attorneys' Bulletin* entitled "Financial Fraud." The Bulletin is issued six times per year and is made available electronically to all USAOs throughout the country. A companion issue containing this Annual Report will be published and distributed in 2011.

A LOOK AHEAD

The TISC will pursue a number of activities to enhance training and information sharing for Task Force members. More specifically, the committee will seek to develop a mechanism by which members can post their upcoming training sessions and modules in a platform accessible to Task Force members and the law enforcement and regulatory community at-large. The committee will also meet with other organizations, such as those agencies which chaired similar committees as part of the National Procurement Fraud Task Force, to learn more about interagency efforts related to information sharing and to identify the strategies that will enhance the work of the Task Force. In order to further increase awareness and to facilitate greater information sharing among Task Force members, the committee will also continue to invite other working group members to participate in TISC meetings. The committee will also expand participation in the *Resource Guide for Financial Investigations* to include new members of the Task Force. Lastly, the TISC will develop a quarterly newsletter in order to provide more regular updates to all Task Force members regarding the work of the overall Task Force.

ENFORCEMENT COMMITTEE

The Enforcement Committee, through its five subject-matter working groups, is tasked with providing collaborative enforcement in priority areas of financial fraud: mortgage fraud, securities and commodities fraud, fraud related to the Recovery Act and other procurement and grant fraud schemes, fraud related to the Troubled Asset Relief Program, and discriminatory conduct.

Mortgage Fraud Working Group

INTRODUCTION

The Mortgage Fraud Working Group (MFWG) was created in November 2009 pursuant to the President's Executive Order establishing the Financial Fraud Enforcement Task Force. The MFWG is co-chaired by: the Department of Justice's (DOJ) Civil Division, represented by Assistant Attorney General Tony West; the Attorney General's Advisory Committee, represented by U.S. Attorney Benjamin Wagner of the Eastern District of California (EDCA); the FBI, represented by Sharon Ormsby, Chief of the Financial Crimes Section; the Department of Housing and Urban Development-Office of the Inspector General (HUD-OIG), represented by Acting Inspector General Michael P. Stephens; and the National Association of Attorneys General, represented by Attorneys General Tom Miller of Iowa and Rob McKenna of Washington. The membership of the MFWG consists of numerous federal components and agencies including DOJ's Criminal and Civil Rights Divisions, the Executive Office for U.S. Attorneys (EOUSA), the Executive Office for U.S. Trustees (EOUST), the Department of Treasury Financial Crimes Enforcement Network (FinCEN), the Internal Revenue Service-Criminal Investigation (IRS-CI), the Federal Deposit

Insurance Corporation (FDIC), the Federal Trade Commission (FTC), the Federal Housing Finance Administration (FHFA), the Securities and Exchange Commission (SEC), the Special Inspector General of the TARP (SIGTARP), the Treasury Department's Office of Financial Stability-Antifraud Unit, the U.S. Postal Inspection Service (USPIS), and the U.S. Secret Service (USSS).

The primary purpose of the MFWG is to increase enforcement in the area of mortgage fraud through greater coordination among law enforcement agencies, to develop and share effective enforcement strategies and regulatory actions and to engage in community outreach and training. As discussed more fully below, to date the MFWG has worked to expand and invigorate the existing local multi-agency mortgage fraud task forces and working groups located in U.S. Attorneys' Offices around the country, to increase both criminal and civil enforcement actions by federal agencies in the near term, and to increase training and other resources available to federal, state and local enforcement agencies going forward.

Demonstrating the effectiveness of the Justice Department's emphasis on combating mortgage fraud, including the enforcement and public outreach efforts of the working group, mortgage fraud prosecutions across the U.S. Attorneys' Offices showed a marked increase in both the volume of cases charged as well as in the severity of the sentences imposed during the Task Force's first year *(See Table 1, page 4.7)*.

OUTREACH AND INITIATIVES

At its initial meeting in December 2009, the MFWG discussed the role of the member agencies regarding the mortgage fraud problem and heard presentations from several members

regarding existing enforcement actions. This meeting also laid the groundwork for conducting regional mortgage fraud summits, organizing nationwide enforcement efforts and providing additional training on how to combat mortgage fraud.

Presentations from Affected Industry Representatives

The MFWG convened a meeting to hear presentations from representatives of the banking industry, a national appraisers association, a non-profit consumer advocacy group and others. The presenters discussed industry reactions to the housing crisis, stepped-up enforcement efforts within the real estate and mortgage finance industries, and the effect of the enactment of the S.A.F.E. Act on industry practices. The group also heard from the non-profit entity NeighborWorks regarding the national Loan Modification Scam Prevention Network.

Regional Mortgage Fraud Summits

In addition to the meeting involving national industry representatives, the MFWG held regional mortgage fraud summits in areas where the mortgage fraud problem is particularly severe. The regional summits were intended to: highlight the nature of the mortgage fraud problem; learn more about the specific nature of mortgage fraud and emerging trends in different parts of the country; and help coordinate and encourage law enforcement agencies to work together.

Miami, Florida (February 24, 2010)

On Febuary 24, 2010, the first regional summit was held at the U.S. Attorney's Office for the Southern District of Florida in Miami. All MFWG co-chairs attended, as did Robb Adkins, Executive Director of the Task Force;

Mortgage Fraud Charging Statistics

	Defendants Charged	Cases Filed	Defendants Terminated	Cases Terminated	Defendants Guilty
FY 2009	526	267	254	106	235
FY 2010	1,235	656	577	303	533

Mortgage Fraud Sentencing Statistics

	Imprisoned 1-12 months	Imprisoned 13-24 months	Imprisoned 25-36 months	Imprisoned 37-60 months	Imprisoned 61+ months
FY 2009	41	43	26	44	37
FY 2010	87	91	60	73	73

Table 1.

Kenneth Donohue, HUD Inspector General; Cindy Guerra, South Florida Deputy Attorney General; James H. Freis Jr., FinCEN Director; Karen Spangenberg, Deputy Assistant Director for the Criminal Division of the FBI; U.S. Attorney Jeffrey Sloman of the Southern District of Florida; and Karin Hoppmann, Executive U.S. Attorney for the Middle District of Florida. The event was attended by representatives of affected industries, real estate professionals, law enforcement and the public. A morning session consisted of two panels of experts who discussed the community impact of mortgage fraud and recent trends. An afternoon session consisted of a two-hour meeting with federal, state and local law enforcement representatives, at which the group discussed best practices, the use of FinCEN and HUD-OIG data, coordination and enforcement actions.

Phoenix, Arizona (March 25, 2010)

The second regional summit was held at the U.S. Courthouse in Phoenix, on March 25, 2010. All MFWG co-chairs attended, as did Task Force Director Robb Adkins; Michael Stephens, HUD Deputy Inspector General; Sharon Ormsby, Chief

of the Financial Crimes Section of the FBI; Susan Segal, Chief Counsel of the Arizona Attorney General's Office, Public Advocacy Division; and U.S. Attorney Dennis Burke of the District of Arizona. Notably, U.S. Attorney General Eric Holder and Arizona Attorney General Terry Goddard were also present.

Two panels discussed mortgage fraud trends in Arizona and the impact on communities and victims. A two-hour meeting was held with federal, state and local law enforcement representatives, at which FinCEN and HUD-OIG made presentations, and the U.S. Trustee addressed the group. There was also discussion of local task force activities, best practices and upcoming enforcement actions.

Detroit, Michigan (April 23, 2010)

A third mortgage fraud summit was held on April 23, 2010, in the U.S. Courthouse in Detroit. All of the co-chairs participated along with Task Force Director Robb Adkins; David Tanay, Chief of the Criminal Division in the Michigan Attorney General's Office; U.S. Attorney Barbara McQuade of the Eastern District of Michigan; James H. Freis

Attorney General Eric Holder speaks at the MFWG regional summit on March 25, 2010, in Phoenix; in back, left to right, are U.S. Attorney Benjamin Wagner (EDCA), AAG Tony West, Arizona Attorney General Terry Goddard, U.S. Attorney Dennis Burke (AZ), and HUD-OIG Deputy Inspector General Michael Stephens.

Jr., FinCEN Director; and other officials. At the Detroit summit, the MFWG again heard from industry and community representatives regarding the impact of mortgage fraud. The members of the working group also held a closed-door session in the afternoon to discuss coordination between federal, state and local law enforcement in the area of mortgage fraud.

Columbus, Ohio (June 2, 2010)

A regional, state-wide mortgage fraud summit was held on June 2, 2010, at the Ohio Supreme Court, in Columbus. The summit was arranged by the U.S. Attorneys' Offices for the Southern and Northern Districts of Ohio, and was attended by U.S. Attorneys Carter Stewart and Steve Dettelbach and Ohio Attorney General Richard Cordray, along with Task Force Director Robb Adkins. The Ohio summit included panels regarding mortgage fraud trends, as well as a panel that included community representatives. The summit also included a closed-door session in the afternoon regarding ongoing law enforcement efforts to combat mortgage fraud.

Fresno and Los Angeles, California (September 29–30, 2010)

The MFWG held another pair of summits in California, first in Fresno on September 29, 2010, and then in Los Angeles on September 30, 2010. All of the MFWG co-chairs attended, as well as Task Force Director Robb Adkins. U.S. Attorney André Birotte of the Central District of California attended the Los Angeles Summit. At each of these summits, the working group again heard from industry and community representatives regarding the devastating impact of mortgage fraud. In the afternoon, the working group held additional meetings with federal, state and local officials regarding various law enforcement matters relating to mortgage fraud.

Operation Stolen Dreams

From early to mid-2010, the working group devoted considerable attention to launching a national mortgage fraud enforcement sweep. The sweep, called Operation Stolen Dreams, lasted from March 1, 2010, to June 18, 2010. During that period, the MFWG worked with federal investigative agencies, U.S. Attorneys' Offices, federal civil enforcement agencies and state attorneys general to maximize federal, state and local criminal mortgage fraud enforcement actions and civil enforcement actions.

On June 17, Attorney General Eric Holder, FBI Director Robert Mueller, HUD Inspector General Ken Donahue, and other law enforcement representatives announced the results of the operation. The sweep surpassed the results of the 2008 Malicious Mortgage Operation and resulted in the following numbers:

CRIMINAL CASES:

Total Number of Arrests: 525

Total Number of Info/Indictments: 863

Total Number of Complaints: 172

Total Number of Convictions: 391

Total Number of Sentencings: 245

Total Number of Defendants Charged,

    Convicted, or Sentenced 1,517

Total Estimated Loss Amount: ..$3.05 billion

CIVIL CASES:

Approximate Number of Defendants: 395

Total Number Civil Enforcement Actions: 191
(including cease and desist actions)

Total Recovered: ....$196.7 million
(including judgments pending approval or suspended and bankruptcy cases)

In addition to the national announcement, a number of U.S. Attorneys' Offices throughout the country held regional events with federal, state and local partners, to announce the local results of the operation.

Public Outreach

The MFWG, in conjunction with the full Task Force, has also engaged in significant public outreach efforts to help combat mortgage fraud. In particular, the Task Force's website at StopFraud.gov serves as a one-stop site for American consumers to learn how to protect themselves from fraud and to report fraud wherever — and however — it occurs. The website contains fraud reporting resources from numerous agencies, including the FTC, HUD, and the U.S. Trustee Program. The website is a valuable source of information regarding mortgage fraud. The Task Force has also partnered with Fannie Mae, Freddie Mac, the Lawyer's Committee and Neighbor-

Works America to support a consumer-friendly website, *www.PreventLoanScams.org*, which supports national, state and local law enforcement efforts to fight mortgage fraud. The website provides an accessible complaint form that can be filled out online and then entered into a national database that serves as a nationwide clearinghouse and destination for loan modification scam information on complaints filed, laws and regulations, and enforcement actions.

Policy Sub-Group

A policy sub-group was established to collectively initiate cross-agency recommendations for policy, procedure, regulation and law changes related to reducing the risk of fraud in the mortgage industry and to improving the effectiveness of anti-fraud measures and investigations. Agency representation includes HUD-OIG, FTC, USSS, FinCEN, Treasury, DOJ, HUD, and FHFA. Projects initiated to date are: FinCEN Suspicious Activity Report (SAR) digital format reporting requirements; use of FHFA "one-off" data from Fannie and Freddie; false statement warnings on mortgage documents; and SAR reporting requirements for non-financial institution mortgage lenders and brokers. In another policy development, the FTC promulgated the Mortgage Assistance Relief Services Rule, which prohibits the advance payment for mortgage assistance relief services as well as deceptive conduct.

TRAINING AND COORDINATION

The MFWG has also devoted significant resources to train law enforcement in the area of combating mortgage fraud, as well as to increase collaboration within the Department of Justice to ensure maximum utilization of law enforcement resources. Additionally, the working group has made more extensive use of civil enforcement tools to combat mortgage fraud.

On March 2-4, 2010, the MFWG, working with the Office of Legal Education and EOUSA, sponsored a three-day Mortgage Fraud Task Force Conference at the National Advocacy Center (NAC) for both federal and state enforcement attorneys. This course, the first of its kind, brought together Assistant U.S. Attorneys (AUSAs), who handle criminal and civil matters, and state and local prosecutors from state attorneys' general offices and district attorneys' offices around the country. The course covered the operation of mortgage fraud task forces, federal-state cooperation and coordination in combating mortgage fraud, civil tools, state tools, case studies and discovery issues. The course also included regional breakout sessions. Approximately 130 attorneys attended the three-day course. MFWG co-chairs Assistant Attorney General Tony West and U.S. Attorney Benjamin Wagner and Task Force Director Robb Adkins each participated as instructors at the course. Other instructors included experienced Criminal Division attorneys, AUSAs, representatives from state attorneys general offices, the FBI, HUD-OIG and FinCEN.

A second mortgage fraud seminar was presented at the NAC on May 25-27, 2010. Additionally, on July 14-16, the NAC held a White Collar Crime Seminar, which included a session focused on mortgage fraud issues.

The May 2010 *USA Bulletin* was devoted to mortgage fraud. The introduction was written by MFWG co-chair Benjamin Wagner, and the issue contained numerous articles addressing various aspects of both criminal and civil mortgage fraud enforcement.

Additionally, at the U.S. Attorneys' national conference in Tempe, Arizona, on March 24, 2010, MFWG co-chairs Assistant Attorney General Tony West and U.S. Attorney Benjamin Wagner participated in a panel presentation to the U.S. Attorneys on the activities of the Task Force. The panel also included Task Force Director Robb Adkins, Criminal Division Assistant Attorney General Lanny Breuer, U.S. Attorney Preet Bharara of the Southern District of New York and Charles Steele, Deputy Director of FinCEN.

The MFWG has also sought mechanisms to help financial institutions more easily identify suspected mortgage fraud. More specifically, members of the MFWG issued two public advisories that contained "red flag" indicators to identify loan modification fraud as well as reverse mortgage fraud perpetrated against senior citizens. Additionally, FinCEN recently published a Notice of Proposed Rulemaking to define non-bank residential mortgage lenders and originators, formerly responsible for more than half of residential mortgage markets, as loan or finance companies for the purpose of requiring them to establish anti-money laundering programs and report suspicious activities under the Bank Secrecy Act.

In April 2010, the Civil Division issued a guidance memorandum to all U.S. Attorneys' Offices concerning civil tools and strategies for use in civil mortgage fraud enforcement cases. This memorandum outlined the various civil tools available to combat mortgage fraud, including the False Claims Act; the Financial Institutions Reform, Recovery and Enforcement Act of 1989; and the Civil Anti-Fraud Injunction Act.

SIGNIFICANT ENFORCEMENT ACTIONS

The following is a summary of just a few of the significant enforcement actions brought by members of the MFGW. Many of these actions were part of Operation Stolen Dreams.

Builder Bailout Scheme in Chico, California

On May 28, 2010, Anthony G. Symmes pleaded guilty to a mail fraud conspiracy and money laundering, in connection with a large-scale builder-bailout mortgage fraud scheme. For many years, Symmes was the largest home builder in Chico, California. In 2006, as the market cooled, Symmes had a significant amount of unsold new homes in inventory. Symmes established relationships with several unlicensed mortgage brokers to "sell" his homes to straw buyers at inflated prices. Typically, the day after escrow closed, Symmes rebated $40,000 to $60,000 of the reported purchase price per home to shell companies controlled by the buyers' agents. The rebates were not disclosed to the lenders. Altogether, from 2006 through 2008, Symmes sold 62 homes with undisclosed sales rebates. The homes were financed in the aggregate amount of $21 million. Dozens of the homes have fallen into foreclosure, causing losses to date of $5 million. Symmes is cooperating in an ongoing mortgage fraud investigation, and has paid $4 million toward restitution. This case was a joint enforcement action involving the U.S. Attorney's Office for the Eastern District of California, FBI, IRS-CI and the Butte County District Attorney's Office.

Miami Mortgage Fraud Case Targeting Haitian-American Community

On June 16, 2010, Yolette Antoine and Constance Powell were arrested and a six-count indictment was unsealed charging them for their roles in a mortgage fraud scheme that resulted in the approval and disbursement of approximately $4.4 million in fraudulent mortgage loans, and losses of approximately $1.5 million to various lenders. Antoine advertised herself in the Haitian-American community as someone who could provide assistance with immigration issues and as the manager of a government-sponsored housing program. When individuals contacted her concerning the immigration assistance or the supposed housing program, Antoine would allegedly obtain their personal identifying information, including the individuals' names, social security numbers and copies of their driver's licenses. The defendants allegedly used this personal information to fraudulently purchase various properties without the permission of the individuals. After the closings for the properties, Antoine would prepare and execute fraudulent quit-claim deeds transferring title in the properties to The Antoine Investment Group. This case involved cooperation between the U.S. Attorney's Office for the Southern District of Florida, USPIS, State of Florida Office of Financial Regulation and the FBI.

Detroit "Ghost Loans" Mortgage Fraud Scheme

On June 16, 2010, Ronnie Edward Duke, William Camsell Wells III, Wilinevah Jacqueline Richardson, Ryan Andrew Zundel, Robert Charles Brierley, Nicole Lynn Turcheck and Anthony Edward Peteres were charged in a criminal complaint for mortgage fraud. From 2003 to 2007, Duke and co-conspirators operated a mortgage fraud scheme to defraud 61 financial institutions throughout the United States. The conspirators posed as mortgage brokers, appraisers, real estate agents and title agents. They recruited more than 108 straw buyers to obtain approximately 500 mortgages on 180 properties resulting in more than $100 million in losses. False information was provided to mortgage companies to enhance the straw buyers' creditworthiness. The crux of the scheme was to place multiple "ghost loans," or unrecorded loans, on one residential property without the other lender's knowledge. This case involved cooperation between the U.S. Attorney's Office for the Eastern District of Michigan and the FBI.

$108 Million Countrywide Settlement

Coordination between the FTC and the Department of Justice's U.S. Trustee Program resulted in a global settlement under which two Countrywide mortgage servicing companies agreed to pay $108 million to settle charges that they: 1) inflated fees charged to cash-strapped homeowners whose mortgages they were servicing; 2) made false or unsupported claims about amounts owed by homeowners in chapter 13 proceedings; 3) failed to properly credit payments from chapter 13 homeowners; 4) failed to notify chapter 13 homeowners of extra charges added to their mortgage bills; and 5) unfairly tried to collect previously undisclosed charges after the homeowners' bankruptcy cases were closed. The FTC consent order resolved its complaint as well as the U.S. Trustee Program's challenges to Countrywide's mortgage servicing practices in bankruptcy court litigation throughout the country. Under the consent order, overcharged homeowners whose loans were serviced by Countrywide before it was acquired by Bank of America in July 2008 will be reimbursed from a $108 million redress fund administered by the FTC; Countrywide will establish internal procedures and an independent third party will verify compliance with the prescribed procedures to help ensure that the claims filed in bankruptcy are accurate; and Countrywide will provide adequate notice of its charges so that homeowners do not emerge from bankruptcy only to be required to pay previously undisclosed charges or risk foreclosure.

New Jersey Scheme Bankrupted Two Companies

Leroy Hayden, the servicing manager of U.S. Mortgage (USM) from 2004 through January 2009, pleaded guilty on May 13, 2010, for his role in the fraudulent sale of more than $136 million in mortgage loans to Fannie Mae and other investors. USM did not actually own the mortgage loans. Michael McGrath Jr., the president of USM, had previously pleaded guilty for his leadership role in this offense, and admitted to diverting the proceeds of those sales to fund USM's operations and for his personal use. The scheme bankrupted USM and its wholly-owned subsidiary, CU National Mortgage LLC. This case involved cooperation between the U.S. Attorney's Office for the District of New Jersey, USPIS, IRS-CI, FBI and HUD-OIG.

Reverse Mortgage Scheme in Atlanta Targeted the Elderly

In 2010, the U.S. Attorney's Office for the Northern District of Georgia prosecuted one of the first reverse mortgage fraud prosecutions in the country, a type of scheme that targets the elderly. This case is also the first prosecution involving alterations to a Multiple Listing Service (MLS) routinely relied upon by appraisers, realtors, tax assessors and others in the mortgage industry to establish accurate property valuations. Defendants Kelsey Hull and Jonathan Kimpson profited from the corruption of a Federal Housing Administration (FHA)-insured program designed to assist seniors 62 years or older with either cash for equity in their homes ("refi reverses"), or with funds toward the purchase of a home ("purchase money reverses"). The defendants faked down payments and arranged inflated appraisals to create bogus equity of up to $100,000 in the properties securing these reverse mortgage loans, while diverting loan proceeds to themselves. Kimpson used the stolen identities and passwords of realtors to increase MLS listing and sale prices in support of inflated appraisals to create the substantial equity used in the properties. Both defendants pleaded guilty on April 8, 2010, in separate cases, to conspiracy to defraud reverse mortgage lenders and the HUD/FHA insurer of the loans. Hull pleaded to an additional count of bank fraud and Kimpson to an additional count of aggravated identity theft. These cases were investigated by HUD-OIG and the FBI, assisted by the USSS, FinCEN, and by local law enforcement including the DeKalb County Police Department, DeKalb County Probation Office and the Cobb County Sheriff's Department.

Federal Trade Commission Civil Enforcement Actions

In 2010, the FTC filed four civil enforcement actions in federal district court against 25 defendants allegedly engaging in mortgage assistance relief scams, including foreclosure rescue scams, loan modification scams and mortgage loan audit scams. These cases include the actions against Fedmortgageloans.com, Residential Relief Foundation, U.S. Homeowners Relief and National Financial Assistance LLC, each of which involved individuals or entities seeking to victimize distressed homeowners with false loan modification scams or fraudulent foreclosure avoidance schemes. In each of these cases the FTC obtained preliminary injunctive relief halting the allegedly deceptive practices and other equitable relief, including asset freezes and/or appointments of receivers to preserve the possibility of consumer redress. In addition, the FTC obtained final orders against 66 defendants in previously filed cases, permanently banning defendants from engaging in mortgage assistance relief services and imposing approximately $82 million in judgments, of which approximately $35.4 million was suspended based upon the defendants' inability to pay. These cases include civil contempt judgment against Bryan D'Antonio and three companies he controls for violating a 2001 order obtained by the FTC against D'Antonio and his former company, Data Medical Capital Inc., as well as the summary judgment against Dinamica Financiera LLC, Valentin Benitez and Jose Mario Esquer in connection with their respective foreclosure rescue scams.

Michael A. Trap, Glenn S. Rosofsky and Roger T. Jones

During 2010, Michael A. Trap, Glen S. Rosofsky and Roger T. Jones pleaded guilty to operating Nations Housing Modification Center (NHMC) as a fraudulent mortgage loan modification business, and defrauding more than 300 distressed homeowners out of more than $900,000 between April and July 2009. The three conspirators fraudulently sold loan modification services by falsely claiming that NHMC had attorneys and forensic accountants on staff to negotiate with banks on behalf of NHMC's customers, that NHMC had achieved an "extremely high success rate for homeowners that met the Nations Home Affordable Modification Program guidelines," and that NHMC was located on Capitol Hill in Washington, D.C. In fact, NHMC did not have attorneys or forensic accountants on staff, did not have a high success rate of modifying loans, had no connection with the U.S. Treasury Department's Making Home Affordable program, and its only presence in Washington, D.C., was a rented post office box. These false claims were made in solicitation letters that were mailed throughout the country to individuals behind on their mortgage payments, and encouraged struggling homeowners to call a toll-free number to purchase NHMC's loan modification services. The staff of telemarketers at NHMC's offices in San Marcos, California, used a script provided by the conspirators to make similar false and misleading statements to potential customers. Trap and Rosofsky further admitted to engaging in money laundering with the proceeds of this wire fraud scheme, and Jones admitted to lying to SIGTARP Special Agents. Jones was sentenced to 33 months in prison, Rosofsky was sentenced to 63 months in prison, and both defendants were ordered to pay restitution to the victims of this telemarketing offense. Trap will be sentenced in 2011. The case was prosecuted by the U.S. Attorney's Office for the Southern District of California with the help of the San Diego District Attorney's Office, IRS-CI and SIGTARP. Additionally, the FTC obtained a civil judgment against Rosofsky and Trap based on the same mortgage modification scheme.

Edward McCusker

Edward G. McCusker and four others were indicted for executing a $14.6 million mortgage foreclosure rescue scheme. Three of the defendants pleaded guilty in 2010. The defendants claimed to be able to assist homeowners at risk for foreclosure by purchasing their homes, renting the home back to the homeowner, and allowing the homeowner to buy the house back after repairing his or her credit. The defendants used false documents to obtain mortgages to purchase the homes from homeowners. Instead of paying the mortgages obtained on the properties, the defendants allowed many of the homes to go into foreclosure and the homeowners lost everything. The defendants include McCusker, an owner of Axxium Mortgage; his wife; two attorneys who recruited victims into the scheme; and a mortgage broker. The case is being prosecuted by the U.S. Attorney's Office for the Eastern District of Pennsylvania and was investigated by the FBI, USPIS and the Pennsylvania Department of Banking.

Liberty Real Estate Mortgage Fraud Scheme

Ten California residents were indicted in June 2010 for their roles in a multi-million dollar mortgage fraud scam. According to the indictment, Hoda Samuel, a licensed real estate broker, was the head of two Elk Grove, California, companies engaged in residential real estate transactions: Liberty Real Estate and Investment Company and Liberty Mortgage Company. Conspirators at Liberty Mortgage Company allegedly prepared loan applications for borrowers that contained false employment information and inflated income. Two defendants, Connie Devers and Dana Faulkner, who were unlicensed by the Department of Real Estate, helped prepare such loan applications. According to the indictment, when a mortgage lender attempted to verify this information by calling the purported employer, the lender often spoke to a Liberty employee or associate who falsely verified the information. According to the indictment, Liberty typically offered sellers $15,000 to $40,000 more than the asking prices for properties. At times the purchase agreements came with addendums that called for the difference between the two prices to be diverted at closing to contracting companies so that the homes could be remodeled and rendered compliant with the Americans with Disabilities Act. In fact, such remodeling was seldom if ever done, and the payments were funneled indirectly back to Liberty clients. Because the addendums calling for these payments were usually withheld both from appraisers and mortgage lenders, the lenders were typically unaware that the true purchase price for each property was below the total amount funded by the lender. According to the indictment, from April 2006 through February 2007, Liberty was involved in approximately 30 residential real estate transactions in which the mortgage lenders were given false information as to the income of the purchasers and/or the value of the homes being purchased. At least 28 of the properties have since gone into foreclosure, resulting in a loss to lenders of more than $5.5 million. Of the 30 properties that are the subject of the indictment, 20 of them were purchased by buyers who bought more than one residence, representing that they intended to live in each. When a single purchaser bought more than one residence, Liberty would typically arrange for the transactions to be handled by separate title companies, and submit the loan applications to separate mortgage lenders. In addition, the purchases would be scheduled to occur close in time to each other so that one purchase would not appear in a credit report run in connection with a subsequent purchase. The case is the result of an extensive investigation by the FBI and IRS-CI, with assistance from the California Department of Real Estate. The U.S. Attorney's Office for the Eastern District of California is prosecuting the case. To date, two defendants have pleaded guilty for their roles in the fraud scheme.

A LOOK AHEAD

Given the constantly evolving trends and types of mortgage fraud seen in various geographic regions of the country, the MFWG plans to hold more training sessions and summits to address newly emerging schemes, with an increased focus on regional-led efforts. The MFWG will continue to concentrate on outreach efforts to help financial institutions more easily identify mortgage fraud through alerts, advisories and other services. Also, the MFWG will continue to discuss ways to improve tools needed to bring civil and criminal mortgage fraud enforcement actions. Finally, the working group also anticipates expanding its enforcement efforts to combat mortgage fraud through coordinated actions between various Task Force members.

Recovery Act, Procurement And Grant Fraud Working Group

INTRODUCTION

The American Recovery and Reinvestment Act of 2009, Pub. L. No. 111-5, 123 Stat. 115 (Febuary 17, 2009) (Recovery Act), represents an unprecedented effort by the federal government to support the American economy. Over the span of roughly two years, the government will have invested $787 billion in American workers and businesses in the hopes of reviving the struggling economy. This substantial investment is divided among three types of relief: tax benefits ($288 billion); contracts, grants and loans ($275 billion); and entitlements ($224 billion). The Recovery Act was designed in recognition of both the need to rapidly infuse stimulus funds into critical segments of the economy, as well as the overall goal that the funds be spent as intended and not fall victim to fraud, waste or abuse.

To match the ambitious goals of the Recovery Act, Congress created a new watchdog organization tasked solely with the responsibility of ensuring that Recovery Act monies are used for their intended purpose. Headed by Chairman Earl Devaney, and with 12 Inspectors General (IGs) as members, the Recovery Accountability and Transparency Board (Recovery Board) represents an innovative effort to prevent fraud from affecting Recovery Act funds. Through its efforts, the Recovery Board has closely monitored the roll-out of the Recovery Act and coordinated with the IGs of all the federal agencies distributing the funds.

The Task Force's Recovery Act, Procurement and Grant Fraud Working Group (working group) is responsible for coordinating a national strategy to draw on all the resources and expertise of the Justice Department, as well as other partner agencies, regulatory authorities and IGs throughout the Executive Branch, to ensure that taxpayer funds are safeguarded from fraud and abuse and that the Recovery Act effort is conducted in an open, competitive and non-discriminatory manner.

The working group is led by its co-chairs: Assistant Attorney General Lanny Breuer for the Criminal Division of the Department of Justice; Assistant Attorney General Christine Varney for the Antitrust Division of the Department of Justice; Chairman of the Recovery Accountability and Transparency Board, Earl Devaney; and representatives of the National Association of Attorneys General. The working group consists of a broad array of members from federal, state and local law enforcement agencies. Importantly, a critical foundation for the working group is the well-developed enforcement framework previously established by the National Procurement Fraud Task Force, which has now been merged into the working group and has been further enhanced by increased coordination in the community of federal and state IGs under the leadership of the Recovery Board.

OUTREACH AND INITIATIVES

There is a generally accepted consensus that, to date, the current wave of stimulus funds has not suffered from an appreciable level of fraud. According to the Recovery Board, the federal government has thus far released nearly $600 billion. The latest total includes approximately $243 billion in tax credits, $179 billion in entitlement benefits and $176 billion in contract, loan and grant spending. Overall, as of January 2011, approximately 75 percent of the Recovery Act's $787 billion has entered the economy.

Notwithstanding the substantial volume of funds now distributed, the number of federal, state and local prosecutions for Recovery Act-related offenses has been relatively low. The relatively low level of fraud detected to date is due in significant part to the continuing efforts of the Recovery Board and the IGs, bolstered by the working group, to prevent fraud from happening in the first place. The Recovery Board has established two first-rate mechanisms for ensuring transparency in the allocation and spending of Recovery Act dollars, as well as for detecting potential abuses before stimulus funds are wasted or fall victim to fraud: (1) a Recovery Operations Center and (2) Recovery.gov, a website that allows for the reporting of potential fraud, waste and abuse.

The Recovery Operations Center, launched in November 2009, is central to the Recovery Board's efforts to keep a close eye on Recovery money and ensure that contracts, grants and loans are subjected to comprehensive scrutiny. The operations facility is a state-of-the-art command center that combines analysis with sophisticated software tools, government data-bases and open-source information to track the flow of stimulus money. Its primary objective is to serve as a focused, intelligence-sharing point for the oversight community.

The operations center uses sophisticated screening and analysis of high-risk recipients to develop risk-based resource tools for the oversight community. The analytical tools have been designed to intercept fraud closer to the front end of the fraud continuum.

The Recovery Board's skilled analysts look for early warning signs of trouble, searching massive amounts of data to identify criminal convictions, lawsuits, tax liens, bankruptcies, risky financial deals, suspension and debarment proceedings, and other problems. They employ business rules commonly used in industry to help pinpoint high-risk factors. Once a problem has been identified, the analysts then perform an in-depth review of the award and provide a report to the appropriate IG Office for further inquiry.

Analysts also review information and complaints received from citizens who phone the hotline service activated on September 28, 2009. In the past year, more than 2,800 calls, emails, faxes and letters from citizens expressing concern about the use of Recovery funds were received, and 164 were forwarded to IGs for additional review. Separately, IGs with Recovery Act funds have established hotlines of their own so that potential fraud can be reported directly to their agencies.

The Recovery Board is helping to share the operations center model with other government agencies. For example, the Recovery Board's staff conducted a successful 30-day fraud pilot project with the Centers for Medicare and Medicaid Services. The demonstration developed solid investigative leads related to schemes to defraud Medicare and Medicaid.

Many high-profile visitors have toured the operations center in the past year, including Vice President Biden. During his April 6, 2010, visit, the Vice President announced that he was delivering "a very clear and unambiguous message ... straight from the Oval Office: not reporting is not acceptable."

The establishment of the working group last year added the full weight of the law enforcement community behind the Recovery Board's efforts. Because it was established at a stage when stimulus funds had yet to be distributed in any significant quantity, the working group focused its early efforts on laying a solid foundation for a coordinated enforcement response as allegations of Recovery Act fraud surfaced and, equally important, on expanding upon the Recovery Board's vigilant fraud prevention and detection effort aimed at stopping frauds before they occur. The working group has made significant strides toward these ends.

TRAINING AND COORDINATION

Perhaps the most visible and influential work done by the working group to date is the group's fraud prevention and detection training effort. These efforts, which draw significantly from the efforts undertaken by the Recovery Board and the IGs of federal agencies with Recovery Act funds, have targeted two key constituencies: (i) professionals at the federal and state levels responsible for detecting, reporting and/or preventing Recovery Act fraud, such as the procurement and grant officials who are awarding and overseeing Recovery Act funds; and (ii) individuals responsible for investigating and prosecuting Recovery Act fraud, including federal and state agents and civil and criminal prosecutors. At the close of 2010, more than 100,000 professionals responsible for awarding and overseeing Recovery Act funds were trained as part of this effort, and these numbers are only continuing to grow. This targeted

fraud prevention and detection effort is one of the largest such efforts in history.

These efforts were punctuated by a flagship training event for agents, auditors and procurement and grant officers, entitled "Focus on Recovery," which was held in mid-November, 2010, in Philadelphia. The conference boasted speakers from the highest levels of the Justice Department and IG community, as well as elected officials, including the Vice President of the United States. The conference was a tremendous success, attracting well over 500 attendees.

To ensure that a lasting emphasis is placed on prevention and detection training, the working group has also spent considerable time this past year coordinating with existing procurement and grant fraud training programs to include a Recovery Act focus. For example, the working group has coordinated with the Federal Law Enforcement Training Center to include Recovery Act training segments in course curricula for its vast array of training programs for federal investigators. These courses are offered at regular intervals throughout each calendar year.

SIGNIFICANT ENFORCEMENT ACTIONS

The working group has also played an important role in supporting and coordinating the many federal, state and local law enforcement entities involved in the Recovery Act effort. In addition to hosting regular, quarterly meetings among its membership to discuss emerging fraud trends and updates, the working group has been proactive in monitoring Recovery Act fraud trends, identifying opportunities for multi-agency enforcement initiatives, and establishing a coordinated enforcement framework for combating Recovery Act fraud.

The working group has also focused on potential enforcement. Working closely with the Recovery Board, the IG community, and the Department of Justice, the working group is tracking information on criminal prosecutions and civil enforcement matters opened and pending in prosecutors' offices that involve Recovery Act funds. This effort allows the working group to: (i) track existing matters and spot emerging fraud trends; (ii) stay attuned to progress in bringing these fraud cases to prosecution; (iii) identify cases that may require additional resources; and (iv) develop new ideas about strategies for addressing particular frauds and potential legislative fixes.

In addition to monitoring fraud trends and existing enforcement efforts, the working group has been proactive in identifying, fostering and coordinating targeted, multi-agency initiatives designed to address particularized Recovery Act fraud schemes and issues. The fraud schemes emerging in the Recovery Act area are typical of the procurement and grant fraud and tax and benefits frauds that white-collar prosecutors have pursued for many years. In response to the importance placed on protecting Recovery Act funds, the working group has put an emphasis on building strong coalitions among agencies to commit the time and resources necessary to vigorously pursue these crimes and to develop cases when any Recovery Act dollars are at issue. Ensuring strong communication and coordination among civil attorneys and criminal prosecutors, the IG community, and state and local authorities, is essential in combating Recovery Act fraud.

Among the most noteworthy of the working group's coordination efforts this year was the formal integration of the well-developed enforcement framework previously established by the former National Procurement Fraud Task Force (NPFTF) into the working group structure. The NPFTF shared the same goal as the working group — to coordinate law enforcement and regulatory partners in combating fraud against government funds. To maximize the working group's efforts and to better leverage the resources of the IG community, the NPFTF was formally merged into the working group in late 2010.

This merger has significantly broadened the focus of, and more importantly, the resources available to, the working group. The merger has broadened the working group's focus to include enforcement issues of procurement and grant fraud, generally, with the recognition that strengthening procurement and grant fraud enforcement will necessarily benefit the working group's goal of fighting specific Recovery Act frauds. The NPFTF's six committees now operate as part of the working group, with their membership attending regular working group meetings and reporting on committee developments, initiatives and plans.

A LOOK AHEAD

In 2011, the working group intends to continue its aggressive detection and monitoring efforts, primarily through the work of the Recovery Board. In addition, as new frauds on Recovery Act funds are detected by working group members or their law enforcement partners, including the IG community, the working group will stand ready to facilitate the investigation and prosecution of Recovery Act fraudsters by its law enforcement members and partners, including the Criminal and Antitrust Divisions of the Justice Department and the nation's U.S. Attorneys' Offices.

Adding to the already substantial capabilities of the working group will be the six committees that were formerly part of the NPFTF: the Grant Fraud Committee (chaired by Cynthia Schnedar, Acting Inspector General of the Department of Justice); the Information Sharing Committee (chaired by Peggy E. Gustafson,

Inspector General of the Small Business Administration); the Legislation Committee (chaired by Brian D. Miller, the Inspector General of the General Services Administration); the Public/Private Sector Outreach Committee (chaired by Eric M. Thorson, Inspector General of the Treasury Department and Brian D. Miller, Inspector General of the General Services Administration); the Suspension and Debarment Committee (chaired by Allison C. Lerner, Inspector General of the National Science Foundation, and Steve A. Linick, Inspector General of the Federal Housing Finance Agency); and the Training Committee (chaired by David C. Williams, Inspector General of the U.S. Postal Service).

The expertise and experience that these committees and their members bring to bear will be of tremendous benefit for the working group as it moves forward in the year ahead.

Rescue Fraud Working Group

INTRODUCTION

The Task Force's Rescue Fraud Working Group (RFWG) is principally focused on training and outreach relative to the Troubled Asset Relief Program (TARP); detection of fraud, waste and abuse; and increasing the robust and aggressive prosecution of crimes related to the TARP ("rescue fraud"). To this end, the RFWG originally developed several goals: (1) improve coordination and information sharing among agencies addressing rescue fraud; (2) enhance our civil and criminal enforcement efforts; and (3) increase training and outreach opportunities for member agencies.

The RFWG is co-chaired by Christy Romero, Acting Special Inspector General for the Troubled Asset Relief Program (SIGTARP); Assistant Attorney General Lanny Breuer for the Criminal

Division of the Department of Justice (DOJ); and Christian Weideman, Chief Counsel for the Office of Financial Stability (OFS) of the Department of the Treasury. In addition to members from the co-chair agencies, the RFWG is made up of representatives from the FBI, the Internal Revenue Service-Criminal Investigation (IRS-CI), the Financial Crimes Enforcement Network (FinCEN), DOJ's Civil Division, the U.S. Postal Inspection Service (USPIS), U.S. Attorneys' Offices, the Federal Deposit Insurance Corporation — Office of the Inspector General (FDIC-OIG), the Securities and Exchange Commission (SEC), the Federal Trade Commission (FTC), the Federal Reserve Board, the Office of Thrift Supervision, the Office of the Comptroller of the Currency, the FDIC, and others.

During 2010, the RFWG made great progress towards achieving the goals developed during its inaugural year, including partnering with working group members as well as state and local agencies throughout the country to coordinate actions on specific investigations, conducting significant outreach activities, and successfully charging many criminal and civil actions on both the federal and state levels.

OUTREACH, TRAINING AND INITIATIVES

The RFWG held two, full member meetings in Washington, D.C., during 2010, as well as multiple strategic meetings among the co-chairs and their respective representatives. During these meetings, the focus has been largely to educate working group members about the TARP programs administered by OFS, to emphasize fraud detection and to identify existing investigations with a nexus to TARP. Consistent with their missions, SIGTARP and OFS participated in outreach and training activities with respect to the TARP as follows.

SIGTARP

Representatives of SIGTARP made more than 50 presentations during 2010 to both government and private industry representatives in numerous venues. These outreach efforts, which continue into 2011, have concentrated on outlining SIGTARP's authority and mission, providing an overview of the programs administered through TARP, and identifying cases currently in agencies' inventory that may have a TARP connection. Outreach conducted during 2010 included: multiple presentations at DOJ's National Advocacy Center to representatives of DOJ and the 94 U.S. Attorneys' Offices throughout the country; dozens of presentations to groups of federal, state and local law enforcement and prosecutors throughout the country; and presentations to professional organizations such as the American Bar Association and state associations for certified public accountants, among many others. Further, SIGTARP Investigations Division members have held countless meetings throughout the country with Assistant U.S. Attorneys and our law enforcement partners to discuss the intricacies of the programs overseen by SIGTARP.

Additionally, SIGTARP and its law enforcement partners have had significant engagement with the media to ensure that SIGTARP's law enforcement efforts are well understood both by the public and by those who would profit criminally from TARP.

OFS

OFS has continued to provide training and outreach to educate the public and practitioners relative to programs being developed and initiated through TARP.

Making Home Affordable (MHA) Nationwide Outreach

Since June 2009, OFS personnel, in partnership with the Department of Housing and Urban Development (HUD), HOPE Now and NeighborWorks America have held 51 nationwide MHA events which served more than 50,000 homeowners and their families. Significant media coverage has helped reach far beyond the number of people who attended these events.

Also, Treasury has organized partner roundtables in every city visited, meeting with nearly 1,000 local and state officials, housing counselors and congressional staff to provide a program update and receive feedback about the program. Finally, event-related training sessions primarily for housing counselors have reached about 10,000 people.

Ad Council MHA PSA Campaign

Through the end of December 2010, the bilingual Ad Council MHA campaign — launched last July — reported the airing nationwide of more than 45,000 television ads and 95,000 radio ads. The television ads alone translate into 48.8 million times adults 18 years of age and older were exposed to the campaign's public service advertisements. The campaign has also included more than 1,100 MHA billboards.

SIGNIFICANT ENFORCEMENT ACTIONS

SIGTARP has developed into a highly sophisticated white collar crime investigative agency. As of February 28, 2011, SIGTARP had 144 ongoing criminal and civil investigations (including investigations relating to executives at 64 financial institutions that applied for and/or received funding under TARP's Capital Purchase Program), most in partnership with other law enforcement agencies. In partnership with other law enforcement agencies, SIGTARP has participated in investigations that have delivered substantial results:

- asset recoveries of $151.8 million, with an additional estimated savings of $555.2 million through fraud prevention;

- 47 individuals and 16 entities subject to civil or criminal actions;

- criminal convictions of 16 defendants for fraud; and

- civil actions naming 12 corporations or other entities as defendants.

SIGTARP's investigations concern suspected TARP fraud, accounting fraud, securities fraud, insider trading, bank fraud, mortgage fraud, mortgage servicer misconduct, fraudulent advance-fee schemes, public corruption, false statements, obstruction of justice, theft of trade secrets, money laundering, perjury to Congress and tax-related offenses. Over the past year, SIGTARP's investigative activity, in partnership with other investigative agencies and the DOJ, has led to several significant developments, as described below.

Colonial BancGroup/Taylor, Bean & Whitaker

On June 15, 2010, the Justice Department's Criminal Division, together with the U.S. Attorney's Office for the Eastern District of Virginia, filed an indictment against Lee Bentley Farkas, former chairman of Taylor, Bean & Whitaker (TBW), charging him with conspiracy to commit bank, wire and securities fraud; and multiple counts of bank fraud, wire fraud and securities fraud. Among other things, Farkas was charged for his role in attempting to steal $553 million from TARP through the fraudulent application of Colonial BancGroup for TARP funds under the Capital Purchase Program (CPP). Farkas perpetuated a massive fraud scheme that resulted in an undisclosed hole in Colonial's books and records, and later caused a false filing by Colonial with the SEC that falsely represented that Farkas had raised $300 million

in private financing for Colonial, a requirement for Colonial to obtain TARP funding. The fraud scheme involved more than $2.9 billion and contributed to the failures of Colonial and TBW in 2009 and victimized numerous other public and private institutions. Subsequently, in April 2011, Farkas was convicted by a jury on all charges for perpetrating the massive fraud scheme. Also in 2011, prior to Farkas' trial, six co-conspirators pleaded guilty for their roles in the fraud scheme. SIGTARP, the FBI, FDIC-OIG, HUD-Office of Inspector General (HUD-OIG), the Federal Housing Finance Agency-Office of the Inspector General and IRS-CI investigated this case.

The Shmuckler Group LLC

On November 18, 2010, Howard Shmuckler was arrested pursuant to a 30-count indictment obtained by the Prince George's County State's Attorney's Office in Maryland. Shmuckler owned and operated Shmuckler Group, a company located in Vienna, Virginia, that purportedly offered mortgage modification services. He was charged with conspiracy, theft and operating a business without a license, all relating to an alleged mortgage modification scam that took advantage of the publicity surrounding the TARP-supported Home Affordable Modification Program (HAMP). According to a related cease and desist order issued by the Maryland Commissioner of Financial Regulation, Shmuckler, along with two other individuals and their affiliated companies, are alleged to have collected more than $1.2 million in upfront fees from 372 Maryland homeowners by falsely promising to persuade banks to modify the terms of the homeowners' mortgages. According to the same order, Shmuckler contracted with Nova Key LLC to market and sell Shmuckler Group loan modification services to homeowners, including advertising that targeted Spanish-speaking homeowners who had obtained subprime mortgages that they could not afford and who had fallen behind on their mortgage payments. According to the order, many of these homeowners subsequently lost their homes to foreclosure. This case resulted from a joint investigation conducted by SIGTARP, the Office of the State's Attorney for Prince George's County, and the Maryland Department of Labor Licensing and Regulation's Financial Regulation Division.

Residential Relief Foundation

On November 17, 2010, pursuant to court order, the FTC halted the operations of the Residential Relief Foundation and affiliated companies and individuals. This action, supported by SIGTARP's investigative efforts, was based on a civil complaint filed by the FTC alleging that the defendants violated federal law by falsely claiming that they would obtain loan modifications and significantly lower mortgage payments for consumers in return for upfront fees. According to the FTC complaint, the Residential Relief Foundation used a logo similar to the Great Seal of the United States and told consumers that it is nearly impossible for homeowners to obtain mortgage modifications on their own. Claiming quick results and a high success rate, the defendants charged a $1,495 up-front fee, advised homeowners to stop making mortgage payments and falsely claimed that reports the defendants created would enable homeowners to obtain the promised results, according to the complaint. In addition, the FTC charged that in marketing debt relief services for credit card debt, the defendants falsely told people they could become debt free in 12 to 36 months, remove late fees and penalties, and reduce debts up to 50%. At the FTC's request, a federal court ordered a halt to the operation, appointed a receiver and froze the defendants' assets, pending trial. The FTC action seeks to stop the defendants' deceptive claims permanently and make them forfeit their ill-gotten gains. SIGTARP provided investigative support in furtherance of the FTC's case. SIGTARP's investigation is ongoing.

Park Avenue Bank

On October 8, 2010, Charles Antonucci, the former president and chief executive officer (CEO) of Park Avenue Bank, pleaded guilty in the U.S. District Court for the Southern District of New York to offenses including securities fraud, making false statements to bank regulators, bank bribery and embezzlement of bank funds. In particular, Antonucci attempted to steal $11 million of TARP funds by, among other things, making fraudulent claims about the bank's capital position. With his guilty plea, Antonucci became the first defendant convicted of attempting to steal from the taxpayers' investment in TARP. Antonucci falsely represented that he had personally invested $6.5 million in Park Avenue Bank to improve its capital position. As Antonucci admitted, however, the funds were actually borrowed from Park Avenue Bank itself and reinvested as part of an undisclosed "round-trip" transaction. This fraudulent transaction was touted by Park Avenue Bank in its application for TARP funds as evidence of its supposedly improving capital position, a key factor regulators considered when awarding TARP funds. In addition, Antonucci admitted to making false representations to bank regulators about the source of the $6.5 million. The U.S. Attorney's Office for the Southern District of New York prosecuted the case and the ongoing SIGTARP investigation is being conducted in partnership with the FBI, U.S. Immigration and Customs Enforcement (ICE), the New York State Banking Department Criminal Investigations Bureau and FDIC-OIG.

Omni National Bank

Omni National Bank was a national bank headquartered in Atlanta with branch offices in seven states. Omni failed and was taken over by the FDIC on March 27, 2009. Before its failure, Omni had applied for, but did not receive, TARP funds under CPP. SIGTARP has participated in several investigations concerning Omni that have led to criminal charges as part of a mortgage fraud task force that includes SIGTARP, the U.S. Attorney's Office for the Northern District of Georgia, FDIC-OIG, HUD-OIG, USPIS and the FBI. On January 14, 2010, Jeffrey Levine, Omni's former executive vice president, pleaded guilty in federal district court to charges of causing material overvaluations of bank assets in the books, reports and statements of Omni. On March 23, 2010, Brent Merriell pleaded guilty in federal district court to charges of making false statements to the FDIC and six counts of aggravated identity theft in connection with a scheme to prompt Omni to forgive $2.2 million in loans. Delroy Davy pleaded guilty on May 11, 2010, in federal district court to charges of bank fraud and conspiracy. On April 1, 2010, Mark Anthony McBride was sentenced to 16 years in prison on charges of conspiracy to commit bank, mail, wire and bankruptcy fraud. On January 5, 2011, Karim W. Lawrence, an officer and employee of Omni, pleaded guilty to charges of corruptly receiving commissions or gifts in exchange for procuring loans. SIGTARP's involvement in the investigations is ongoing.

United Law Group

In March 2010, SIGTARP, along with USPIS, FBI, ICE and the Orange County District Attorney's Office, executed a publicly filed search warrant obtained by the U.S. Attorney's Office for the Central District of California at the offices of United Law Group (ULG). This investigation focuses on allegations that ULG, taking advantage of the publicity surrounding HAMP, engaged in a mortgage modification advance-fee scheme. The search warrant affidavit alleges that ULG charged struggling homeowners fees ranging from $1,500 to $12,000 without performing services, while advising victims to stop paying their mortgages and terminate contact with their lenders. Many

ULG customers subsequently lost their homes to foreclosure. On June 30, 2010, ULG filed for bankruptcy protection. On December 20, 2010, as a direct result of SIGTARP's investigative efforts, U.S. Bankruptcy Judge Robert Kwan issued a preliminary injunction assigning control of a bank account held by ULG containing client funds to ULG's bankruptcy trustee. The bankruptcy trustee assigned to wind down the operations of ULG in Irvine, California, estimates that approximately $1 million from the seized account will be returned to the estate to serve as restitution to victims. SIGTARP's investigation with its law enforcement partners is ongoing.

Bank of America

On February 4, 2010, the New York Attorney General charged Bank of America Corporation, its former CEO Kenneth D. Lewis, and its former chief financial officer Joseph L. Price, with civil securities fraud. According to the allegations, in order to complete a merger between Bank of America and Merrill Lynch & Co. Inc., the defendants failed to disclose to shareholders spiraling losses at Merrill Lynch. Additionally, after the merger was approved, it is alleged that Bank of America made misrepresentations to the federal government in order to obtain tens of billions of dollars in TARP funds. The investigation was conducted jointly by the New York Attorney General's Office and SIGTARP, and the case remains pending in New York state court.

SIGTARP also assisted the SEC with its Bank of America investigation. On February 22, 2010, U.S. District Judge for the Southern District of New York Jed S. Rakoff, approved a $150 million civil settlement between the SEC and Bank of America to settle all outstanding SEC actions against the firm. The court found that Bank of America failed to disclose adequately to its shareholders, prior to their approval of a merger with Merrill Lynch, the extent of additional material losses that Merrill

Lynch had suffered. Additionally, the court found that the proxy statement sent to shareholders in November 2008 failed to disclose adequately Bank of America's agreement to allow the payment of bonuses to Merrill Lynch employees prior to the merger. In addition to the $150 million payment, Bank of America also agreed to the following settlement requirements:

+ engaging an independent auditor to assess and report on the effectiveness of the company's disclosure controls and procedures;

+ furnishing management certifications signed by the chief executive officer and chief financial officer with respect to proxy statements;

+ retaining disclosure counsel to the audit committee of the company's board of directors;

+ adopting independence requirements beyond those already applicable for all members of the compensation committee of the company's board of directors;

+ retaining an independent compensation consultant to the compensation committee;

+ implementing and disclosing written incentive compensation principles on the company's website and providing the company's shareholders with an advisory vote concerning any proposed changes to such principles; and

+ providing the company's shareholders with an annual "say on pay" advisory vote regarding the compensation of executives.

Mount Vernon Money Center

On March 11, 2010, Robert Egan, president, and Bernard McGarry, chief operating officer, of the Mount Vernon Money Center (MVMC), were indicted in the Southern District of New York on charges related to their theft of more than $50 million entrusted to MVMC. On September 15, 2010, Egan pleaded guilty to conspiracy to commit bank fraud and wire fraud. On October 13, 2010, McGarry pleaded guilty to the same offenses. Egan and McGarry defrauded MVMC clients, including banks that had received TARP funds, out of more than $50 million that had been entrusted to MVMC. MVMC engaged in various cash management businesses, including replenishing cash in more than 5,300 automated teller machines owned by financial institutions. From 2005 through February 2010, Egan and McGarry solicited and collected hundreds of millions of dollars from MVMC's clients on the false representations that they would not co-mingle clients' funds or use the funds for purposes other than those specified in the various contracts with their clients. Relying upon the continual influx of funds, Egan and McGarry misappropriated the clients' funds for their and MVMC's own use, to cover operating expenses of the MVMC operating entities, to repay prior obligations to clients, or for their own personal enrichment. This case was jointly investigated by SIGTARP and the FBI and was prosecuted by the U.S. Attorney's Office for the Southern District of New York.

American Home Recovery

On August 11, 2010, the U.S. District Court for the Southern District of New York unsealed an indictment charging Jaime Cassuto, David Cassuto and Isaak Khafizov, the principals of American Home Recovery (AHR), a mortgage modification company located in New York City, with one count of conspiracy to commit mail and wire fraud, one count of wire fraud, and two counts of mail fraud, all relating to a mortgage modification scam.

The defendants had been arrested in June 2010, on charges contained in a criminal complaint by special agents from SIGTARP and the FBI, as part of the Task Force's nationwide Operation Stolen Dreams mortgage fraud sweep. According to the indictment, the defendants perpetrated a scheme to defraud homeowners using mailings and telemarketing efforts. It is alleged that the defendants, through AHR, falsely promised to assist desperate homeowners by negotiating with banks to modify the terms of their mortgages in exchange for upfront fees of several thousand dollars. In fact, the indictment alleges, AHR did little or no work to modify the mortgages. Through their scheme, the defendants obtained more than $500,000 from homeowners throughout the country, according to the indictment. The indictment further alleges that one of the defendants, Khafizov, directed AHR salespeople to falsely inform prospective clients that AHR had an 80%-90% success rate in securing modification of clients' mortgages and that AHR would issue a full refund of the upfront fee to any client whose mortgage was not successfully modified by AHR. In addition, AHR salespeople allegedly misrepresented to homeowners that AHR would ensure their participation in the TARP-funded MHA program. AHR salespeople falsely advised homeowners that they were more likely to obtain a mortgage modification from their bank if they fell further behind on their mortgage payments and/or stopped making payments to their bank entirely, and sent their money to AHR instead, the indictment alleges. The case is pending. This ongoing SIGTARP investigation is being conducted in partnership with the FBI and is being prosecuted by the U.S. Attorney's Office for the Southern District of New York.

Goldwater Bank

On September 15, 2010, Goldwater N.A., located in Scottsdale, Arizona, entered into a settlement agreement with the U.S. Attorney's Office for the Southern District of New York requiring it to forfeit $733,805 to resolve civil forfeiture claims related to Goldwater's alleged laundering of illegal online gambling proceeds. Goldwater had received approximately $2.6 million from TARP through CPP. Between January and May 2009 more than $13.3 million in funds traceable to offshore online gambling companies were deposited in a bank account at Goldwater held by Allied Wallet Inc. The forfeiture amount equaled the net income that Goldwater received to process these transactions. Additionally, in order to safeguard the government's continued TARP investment in the bank, Goldwater agreed to develop and implement internal anti-money laundering procedures, to comply with the Bank Secrecy Act, and to create internal training programs and an independent audit function to ensure that its compliance is effective. SIGTARP jointly investigated Goldwater with the FBI and the U.S. Attorney's Office for the Southern District of New York.

A LOOK AHEAD

During 2011, the RFWG will continue to focus on training and outreach relative to TARP as well as on the detection of fraud, waste and abuse, and its members will concentrate on the robust and aggressive investigation and prosecution of crimes related to TARP.

Securities and Commodities Fraud Working Group

INTRODUCTION

When the President created the Task Force in November 2009, a central enforcement priority was securities, commodities and investment fraud. To address this priority area, the Securities and Commodities Fraud Working Group (SCFWG) was created to collaborate and exchange information regarding a number of subjects relevant to the work of its members, including developing criminal trends, new laws and regulations, and law enforcement issues and techniques.

The SCFWG is chaired by David Meister, Director of Enforcement for the Commodity Futures Trading Commission (CFTC); Assistant Attorney General Lanny Breuer for the Criminal Division of the Department of Justice; Robert Khuzami, Director of Enforcement for the Securities and Exchange Commission (SEC); and Preet Bharara U.S. Attorney for the Southern District of New York; and includes more than a dozen fraud enforcement agencies and regulators.

OUTREACH AND INITIATIVES

Between December 2009 and December 2010, the SCFWG formally met on four occasions. During these meetings, SCFWG members conducted workshops on, and discussed, a number of important issues related to securities and commodities fraud enforcement, including the Dodd-Frank Wall Street Reform and Consumer Protection Act, the investigation and prosecution of investment frauds, parallel criminal and civil proceedings, and the use of SEC administrative proceedings.

Apart from the formal meetings of the working group, SCFWG representatives communicate regularly to coordinate on specific investigations and prosecutions, as well as relevant policies. SCFWG members also participate in regional cooperative efforts, such as the Virginia Financial and Securities Task Force; the Connecticut Securities, Commodities, and Investor Fraud Task Force; and the South Florida Securities and Investment Fraud Initiative.

Training and Coordination

Each of the formal SCFWG meetings involved training and education opportunities,

and all of the SCFWG members contributed in this area. In addition, SCFWG members have made efforts to educate the law enforcement community and public at large on securities and commodities fraud-related issues. Representative examples come from the CFTC, the Federal Trade Commission (FTC) and the U.S. Postal Inspection Service (USPIS).

Commodity Futures Trading Commission

The CFTC has worked to promote coordination of enforcement efforts with SCFWG members and other law enforcement agencies at the national, regional, state and local levels to address commodities violations, securities violations, market manipulation, corporate fraud and other related financial wrongdoing.

The CFTC's Division of Enforcement meets regularly with the Department of Justice concerning parallel proceedings. The CFTC has also detailed attorneys from its Division of Enforcement to assist the Department of Justice in the criminal investigation and prosecution of commodities fraud. In addition to participating in national financial fraud enforcement working groups, the CFTC has partnered with various regional groups comprised of SCFWG members and state and local civil and criminal authorities. For example, the CFTC is a member of the South Florida Securities and Investment Fraud Initiative, the Virginia Financial and Securities Task Force, the Indiana Financial Crimes Working Group, the Missouri Securities and Commodities Fraud Working Group, the Arizona Securities Investment Working Group, and the Connecticut Securities and Commodities Working Group.

The CFTC has provided training to many SCFWG members and participated in speaker panels and seminars to promote cooperative enforcement efforts on conducting parallel criminal and civil prosecutions of commodities market manipulation and fraud. For example, the CFTC provided training at the Justice Department's National Advocacy Center, the Financial Crimes Division of the FBI and U.S. Attorneys' Offices around the nation. The CFTC has worked with the Department of Justice and the SEC to conduct cross-agency training, especially training involving the CFTC's new enforcement powers under the Dodd-Frank Wall Street Reform and Consumer Protection Act.

Federal Trade Commission

The FTC engaged in several efforts to educate the law enforcement community as well as the public. For example:

◆ *ftc.gov/moneymatters:* To help people affected by the economic downturn, the FTC created ftc.gov/moneymatters, a website with information on how to avoid scams, managing money and dealing with debt. The FTC produced several videos and publications to provide timely and relevant information for consumers facing financial hardship. One video, "Don't Pay for a Promise," offers information for job hunters about recognizing and avoiding job placement scams. Another, "Fraud: An Inside Look," describes bogus investment offers and features a former convicted scammer, and "10 Things You Can Do to Avoid Fraud," is a practical tip sheet on avoiding common frauds and scams.

U.S. Postal Inspection Service

During 2010, USPIS Inspectors educated consumers about various fraud schemes and provided useful tips on how they can protect themselves from being victimized. In addition to conducting regular consumer awareness activities in local communities, USPIS Inspectors also participate in the annual National Consumer Protection Week Campaign, sponsored by the FTC.

In response to an increase in fraud schemes during the economic downturn, the USPIS developed a website, deliveringtrust.com, to provide consumer awareness and fraud prevention tips. As part of the Delivering Trust Campaign, USPIS developed a fraud prevention brochure with additional fraud prevention and awareness tips and mailed it to every household in the United States.

SIGNIFICANT ENFORCEMENT ACTIONS

During 2010, SCFWG members investigated, filed charges, obtained convictions, and secured lengthy jail sentences in numerous significant cases involving securities, commodities and other investment frauds. What follows are examples of these efforts.

Commodity Futures Trading Commission

The CFTC has devoted considerable efforts to partnering with SCFWG members to address and deter conduct that violates the Commodity Exchange Act (CEA), 7 U.S.C. § 1 *et seq.*, and the CFTC Regulations, 17 C.F.R. § 1.1 *et seq.*, including unlawful market manipulation, commodity pool/hedge fund fraud and illegal off-exchange commodity schemes.

During Fiscal Year (FY) 2010 (ending September 30, 2010), more than 95 percent of the CFTC's major injunctive fraud cases involved related criminal investigations and, as of February 2011, more than 65 percent of those investigations resulted in criminal charges. The CFTC also engaged in cooperative enforcement efforts with civil regulatory SCFWG members during FY 2010, and approximately 65 percent of the CFTC's major fraud actions involved parallel investigations with federal civil authorities.

The CFTC filed 57 enforcement actions in FY 2010, representing a 14 percent increase over the number of cases filed in FY 2009. The CFTC's filings involved allegations of market manipulation, including false reporting and false statements, fraud, registration abuses and other violations of the CEA. During FY 2010, the CFTC obtained judgments ordering the payment of more than $200 million in civil monetary penalties, restitution and disgorgement. During FY 2010, the CFTC opened 419 investigations, which represented 66 percent more than the 251 investigations opened in FY 2009.

The following are examples of significant CFTC enforcement actions in 2010:

Market Manipulation, False Reporting and Trade Practice Violations

◆ In re Moore Capital Mgmt. L.P., et al.

On April 29, 2010, the CFTC simultaneously filed and settled an administrative action against Moore Capital Management LP (MCM) and two of its affiliates. The order found that, since at least November 2007 through May 2008, a former MCM portfolio manager attempted to manipulate the settlement prices of the New York Mercantile Exchange (NYMEX) platinum and palladium futures contracts by engaging in a practice known as "banging the close." The order also found that MCM failed to diligently supervise the handling of MCM's commodity interest business. The CFTC issued a cease and desist order and imposed a $25 million civil monetary penalty, three-year registration prohibition and an order to comply with certain trading undertakings.

◆ In re Morgan Stanley Capital Group Inc.; In re UBS Securities LLC

On April 29, 2010, the CFTC simultaneously filed and settled an administrative enforcement action against Morgan Stanley Capital Group Inc. in connection with Morgan Stanley concealing from the NYMEX the existence of a large Trade at Settlement block crude oil trade. The CFTC also simultaneously filed and settled an administrative enforcement action against UBS Securities on the same day for aiding and abetting that concealment. The order found that the actions of Morgan Stanley and UBS Securities concealed the occurrence of the trade from the NYMEX. The CFTC order required Morgan Stanley to pay a $14 million civil monetary penalty, cease and desist from further violations of the CEA, and comply with certain trading undertakings. The CFTC ordered UBS Securities to pay a $200,000 civil monetary penalty and to cease and desist from violations of the CEA. The CFTC received cooperation from the New York County District Attorney's Office in connection with this matter.

◆ In re ConAgra Trade Group Inc.

On August 16, 2010, the CFTC simultaneously filed and settled an administrative enforcement action against ConAgra Trade Group Inc. (CTG) finding that CTG caused a non-bona fide price to be reported in the NYMEX crude oil futures contract on January 2, 2008. Specifically, the order finds that on January 2, 2008, CTG was the first to purchase NYMEX crude oil futures contracts at the then-historic price of $100; as a result, CTG caused a non-bona fide price to be reported. The CFTC assessed sanctions, including: a $12 million civil monetary penalty; a cease and desist order; and an order to comply with certain undertakings regarding its compliance and ethics program, including appointing an independent person to the Board of Directors, forming a Compliance Committee of the Board and providing enhanced compliance training. The CFTC received cooperation from the NYMEX in connection with this matter.

Commodity Pool/Hedge Fund Fraud

♦ **In re Riley and Pressio Capital Management**

On February 18, 2010, the CFTC simultaneously filed and settled an administrative enforcement action against Craig A. Riley and his firm, Pressio Capital Management LP. The CFTC issued an order finding that the defendants engaged in commodity pool fraud involving the solicitation of more than $3 million from approximately 19 individuals. The order found that defendants made misrepresentations and issued false account statements to pool participants to conceal trading losses and misappropriations. The CFTC order imposed a cease and desist order, permanent trading and registration bans, and a $1 million civil monetary penalty. In a related criminal action filed by the U.S. Attorney's Office for the Central District of California, Riley pleaded guilty to fraud in connection with a scheme to defraud or obtain money or property by means of materially false pretenses and was sentenced to 41 months in prison and ordered to pay $3,044,384 in restitution.

♦ **CFTC v. Lake Dow LLC, et al.**

On March 25, 2010, the U.S. District Court for the Northern District of Georgia ordered Lake Dow Capital LLC and Ty Edwards to pay more than $4 million in restitution and civil monetary penalties. The order found that the defendants committed fraud in operating the Aurora Investment Fund, a commodity pool and hedge fund, which fraudulently solicited more than $26 million from customers and misappropriated customer funds.

♦ **CFTC v. Enrique F. Villalba Jr.**

On March 29, 2010, the CFTC filed a civil injunctive action in the U.S. District Court for the Northern District of Ohio charging Enrique F. Villalba Jr. and his firm, Money Market Alternative LP, with operating a $37.5 million commodity futures Ponzi scheme. The complaint charged that defendants misappropriated at least $3 million in investor funds and allegedly used more than $7 million of investor funds to make Ponzi-style payments to new and existing investors. The CFTC received cooperation from the U.S. Attorney's Office for the Northern District of Ohio and the SEC in connection with this matter.

Foreign Currency Exchange (Forex) Fraud

♦ **CFTC v. Robert Mihailovich Sr.,** *et al.*

On July 27, 2010, the CFTC filed a civil injunctive action in the U.S. District Court for the Northern District of Texas charging Robert Mihailovich Sr. and Growth Capital Management LLC, with fraudulent solicitation in connection with a fraudulent forex scheme. The CFTC's complaint alleged that the defendants fraudulently solicited and accepted more than $30 million from more than 90 customers to engage in futures and forex transactions. According to the complaint the defendants made false representations about their trading expertise and trading record. The CFTC received cooperation from the SEC and the National Futures Association in connection with this matter.

◆ **CFTC v. Cook, *et al.***

On September 28, 2010, the U.S. District Court for the District of Minnesota entered a judgment against Trevor Cook, Patrick Kiley, and their companies, Oxford Global Advisors LLC, Oxford Global Partners LLC, Universal Brokerage FX and Universal Brokerage FX Diversified. The CFTC complaint alleged that the defendants engaged in a massive forex scheme that defrauded 1,000 customers of more than $190 million. In related actions, the U.S. Attorney's Office for the District of Minnesota obtained a criminal indictment against Cook for fraud and related charges and the SEC filed a complaint against Cook charging him with securities fraud. On August 20, 2010, Cook was sentenced to 25 years in prison and ordered to pay $158 million in restitution. The CFTC received cooperation from the U.S. Attorney's Office for the District of Minnesota and the SEC.

◆ **CFTC v. Trader's International Return Network, *et al.***

On September 8, 2010, the U.S. District Court for the Middle District of Florida entered a judgment against Trader's International Return Network (TIRN) and its president, David Merrick, for solicitation fraud, and misappropriation of customer funds involving a purported forex investment program. The court found that the defendants accepted at least $16.4 million from customers to participate in TIRN's investment program, made false representations about how the funds were invested and misappropriated funds for various purposes. The CFTC received cooperation from the SEC and the U.S. Attorney's Office for the Middle District of Florida in connection with this matter.

The Criminal Division, Department of Justice

The Fraud Section of the Justice Department's Criminal Division has made significant contributions to the Task Force's nationwide effort to bring to justice those who commit financial fraud. Fraud Section trial attorneys investigate and prosecute cases throughout the country and across transnational borders involving those who engage in market manipulation, investment fraud, corporate fraud, commodities and securities fraud. The following cases illustrate how the Fraud Section has combated these types of abuses in the securities markets in 2010:

Market Manipulation

◆ On January 28, 2010, Phillip W. Offill Jr., a securities lawyer from Dallas, who had previously been an enforcement and trial attorney for 15 years with the Fort Worth Office of the SEC, was convicted on one count of conspiracy to commit securities registration violations in connection with nine companies. He was also convicted of conspiracy to commit securities fraud and wire fraud in connection with three of those companies and nine counts of wire fraud. Offill participated in a multi-million dollar pump-and-dump stock manipulation scheme. He was sentenced in April 2010 to 96 months in prison. The U.S. Attorney's Office for the Eastern District of Virginia also participated in the prosecution. The FBI and USPIS investigated the case.

◆ On October 29, 2010, George David Gordon, a securities attorney, and Richard Clark, a businessman and former stock broker, were sentenced on charges stemming from a scheme to defraud investors through the "pump-and-dump" manipulation of publicly traded stocks of three companies.

Gordon and Clark were convicted at trial in May 2010. Evidence at trial established that they obtained approximately $43 million in proceeds from the stock manipulation. Gordon was sentenced to 188 months in prison and Clark was sentenced to 151 months in prison. The U.S. Attorney's Office for the Northern District of Oklahoma also participated in the prosecution. The case was investigated by Internal Revenue Service-Criminal Investiga-tion (IRS-CI), the FBI and USPIS.

Investment Fraud

◆ In September 2010, three principals of A&O entities, a group of businesses that acquired and marketed life settlements to investors, were indicted for their alleged roles in a $100 million fraud scheme. Christian M. Allmendinger, Adley H. Abdulwahab and David C. White were charged for defrauding investors by making misrepresentations about such things as A&O's prior success, its size and office locations, the risks of its investment offerings and its safekeeping and use of investor funds. Their fraud scheme involved more than 800 victims throughout the United States and Canada, many of whom were elderly. The indictment also alleged that Allmendinger, Abdulwahab and their co-conspirators routinely used investor funds for personal enrichment. Subsequently, in February 2011, White pleaded guilty to, and in March 2011, Allmendinger was convicted at trial of, conspiracy, mail fraud, money laundering and securities fraud.

Four defendants pleaded guilty in 2010 for their roles in the A&O fraud scheme: Tomme Bromseth, an independent sales agent; Brent P. Oncale, A&O Resource Management Ltd. owner and operator; attorney Russell E. Mackert; and Eric Kurz. The cases are being prosecuted jointly by the Criminal Division and the U.S. Attorney's Office for the Eastern District of Virginia and investigated by the Virginia Financial and Securities Fraud Task Force, which includes the USPIS, IRS-CI and the FBI.

Corporate Fraud

◆ On June 15, 2010, Lee Bentley Farkas, the former chairman of a private mortgage lending company, Taylor Bean & Whitaker (TBW), was arrested and charged in an indictment with conspiracy to commit bank, wire, and securities fraud, and multiple counts of bank fraud, wire fraud, and securities fraud in connection with a more than $2.9 billion fraud scheme that contributed to the failures of Colonial Bank and TBW. This is one of the largest cases in the nation involving the use of fraudulent accounting in connection with mortgage-backed securities and one of the largest bank fraud schemes in the country. Subsequently, in April 2011, Farkas was convicted by a jury on all charges for perpetrating the massive fraud scheme. Also in 2011, prior to Farkas' trial, six co-conspirators pleaded guilty for their roles in the fraud scheme. The U.S. Attorney's Office for the Eastern District of Virginia also participated in the prosecution. The case was investigated by the Office of the Special Inspector General for the Troubled Asset Relief Program (SIG-TARP), the FBI, the Federal Deposit Insurance Corporation-Office of the Inspector General, the Department of Housing and Urban Development-Office of the Inspector General, the Federal Housing Finance Agency-Office of the Inspector General, and IRS-CI.

Commodities Fraud

◆ On June 8, 2010, in the Northern District of Texas, Ray M. White, who operated CRW Management LP (CRW), based in Mansfield, Texas, pleaded guilty to commodities fraud charges stemming from an off-exchange forex trading investment scheme. White received in excess of $7 million from investors, which he in turn used primarily to purchase homes and automobiles, and to support other family business operations. White specifically admitted that in July 2008 he contracted with an investor to sell $50,000 in commodities through CRW. White represented to the investor that his funds would be used to trade off-exchange forex contracts and that CRW averaged seven percent per week returns through off-exchange forex trading. White also admitted that he provided false written account statements showing purported returns and represented to this investor that CRW would maintain separate bank accounts for each investor. White admitted that he either misappropriated investor funds or paid them to other investors. White admitted losing more than $86,500 on off-exchange forex trading, rather than making the seven percent per week profits he claimed on the moneys he received. The case is being jointly prosecuted by the Criminal Division and the U.S. Attorney's Office for the Northern District of Texas. The CFTC, the SEC, the FBI and USPIS investigated the case.

♦ In December 2010, David Lewalski was indicted for his alleged participation in a $30 million investment scheme involving investments in the forex market. The indictment alleges that Lewalski solicited money from investors in Florida and throughout the country based on false statements that he could earn them up to 10 percent interest per month through forex trading. He allegedly invested only a small portion of the investor funds in trading activities and generated little if any profits trading foreign currency. Court documents allege that Lewalski and his co-conspirators made "interest payments" to investors using other investors' money. The Criminal Division and the U.S. Attorney's Office for the Middle District of Florida are prosecuting the case.

The case was investigated by USPIS and the Florida Department of Law Enforcement.

The Department of Labor

The Department of Labor's (DOL) Employee Benefits Security Administration (EBSA) conducts investigations of criminal violations regarding fraud in connection with employee benefit plans such as embezzlement, kickbacks and false statements. During 2010, EBSA investigated several significant cases in this area, including the following:

♦ **United States v. Fuqua**

On November 29, 2010, Knox H. Fuqua was sentenced to 12 months in prison for embezzling money from an employee benefit plan. Fuqua was a financial advisor who also served as trustee of the Community Health Systems Inc. (CHS) 401(k) plan. In June 2005, Fuqua transferred $600,000 from the 401(k) plan to a CHS bank account and immediately used these funds to purchase two certificates of deposit (CD) in the name of a fixed-income fund that he controlled. Fuqua then used these CDs as collateral for a $600,000 line of credit on behalf of the fixed-income fund, and thereafter transferred this amount to another Fuqua client that had requested the liquidation of its interest in the fixed-income fund. DOL investigated this matter with IRS-CI, USPIS and it was prosecuted by the U.S. Attorney's Office for the Southern District of West Virginia.

♦ **United States v. Rogelio Ibanez Jr.**

On April 14, 2010, Rogelio Ibanez Jr., an attorney who lived in Mission, Texas, was indicted on six counts of wire fraud and five counts of theft or embezzlement from an employee benefit plan. Ibanez was the plan administrator and trustee for a title company's 401(k) plan. Accordingly, he was responsible for ensuring that the 401(k) plan was operated for the exclusive benefit of the participants and their beneficiaries. Ibanez withheld funds from employees' paychecks, employee 401(k) contributions, health insurance premiums, and life insurance premiums but failed to remit several thousand dollars to these plans for the benefit of the participants. DOL conducted this investigation with the FBI, the Texas Department of Insurance and various other state and local law enforcement agencies. It was prosecuted by the U.S. Attorney's Office for the Southern District of Texas.

◆ United States v. Anthony A. James

On September 9, 2010, Anthony A. James, an investment advisor who operated James Asset Advisory LLC (a Michigan corporation), was sentenced in federal district court to 163 months in prison followed by 60 months of supervised release. The court also ordered James to pay $2,667,762 in restitution to his victims. James was convicted on April 15, 2010, on seven counts of mail fraud, six counts of wire fraud and one count of embezzlement from an employee benefit plan. From 2001 through June 2009, Anthony James received over $5,300,000 from more than 40 investors, among them contributory ERISA-covered employee benefit plans. James told his clients that he would invest their funds in securities, bonds and mutual funds for their benefit. He would then create individualized asset allocation reports suggesting investment options, backed by bogus quarterly account statements which tracked the investors' money as if it had actually been invested. Instead of investing their money, however, he spent approximately $2,500,000 for his personal use and paid out approximately $2,800,000 to prior investors. DOL conducted this investigation

with the FBI. The U.S. Attorney's Office for the Eastern District of Michigan prosecuted the case.

◆ United States v. Rhonda Sue Irvin Cox

On July 15, 2010, Rhonda Sue Irvin Cox, president and owner of a third party plan administrator firm, was charged with embezzlement from an employee benefit plan, and making false statements in relation to documents required by Employee Retirement Income Security Act (ERISA). Cox illegally embezzled funds through 401(k) rollovers, conversions and contributions in excess of $700,000 from 12 of the 56 employee retirement plans that she administered. As a result of her actions, hundreds of individual participants across the United States suffered losses. On February 14, 2011, Cox pleaded guilty. DOL investigated this matter with the Warren County Sheriff's Office in Lebanon, Ohio. The case was prosecuted by the U.S. Attorney's Office for the Southern District of Ohio.

Federal Bureau of Investigation

The FBI investigates matters relating to fraud, theft or embezzlement occurring within or against the national and international financial community. The FBI focuses its financial crimes investigations in a number of areas, including securities and commodities fraud. In 2010, the FBI participated in many of the SCFWG matters discussed herein. The following highlights several of its significant contributions in this area:

◆ Petters Group Worldwide LLC

Thomas J. Petters used a successful corporation for more than a decade to perpetrate a ponzi scheme that defrauded hundreds of investors of $3.4 billion. This case was the largest fraud case prosecuted in the state of Minnesota.

Petters, through his companies, Petters Group Worldwide LLC (PGW) and Petters Company Inc. (PCI), obtained loans from hedge funds and investment groups for the stated purpose of financing sales to well known big box retailers, such as Costco and Sam's Club. The investigation revealed that the purchase and subsequent sale of merchandise to the retailers were actually fabricated transactions supported by fictional documentation.

As discussed below, the U.S. Attorney's Office for the District of Minnesota secured an indictment against Petters for mail and wire fraud, conspiracy, and money laundering in December 2008. On Dececember 2, 2009, following trial, Petters was convicted on all counts. On April 8, 2010, Petters was sentenced to 50 years in prison, one of the longest financial crimes-related sentences in history. In addition, co-conspirators Deanna Coleman, Robert White, Larry Reynolds, Michael Catain, James Wehmhoff, Greg Bell and Harold Katz were each sentenced to prison in 2010. During 2010, the U.S. Attorney's Office for the District of Minnesota, the FBI and other SCFWG members continued their investigation into the Petters ponzi scheme and several PCI hedge fund investors.

◆ **Scott Rothstein**

On January 27, 2010, Scott Rothstein, an attorney with Rothstein, Rosenfeldt, & Adler (RRA) in Florida, pleaded guilty in the Southern District of Florida to running a $1.2 billion Ponzi scheme involving the sale of shares in purported insurance settlements with guaranteed rates of return on the investments. In actuality, there were no settlements. As part of his guilty plea, Rothstein agreed to relinquish 22 properties,

a dozen cars, a yacht and interest in 100 business entities. On June 11, 2010, Debra Villegas, former chief operating officer of RRA, pleaded guilty for her supporting role in this scheme. She created false documentation to help Rothstein sell investment opportunities and later assisted him with laundering the illicit proceeds. On December 8, 2010, Villegas was sentenced to 10 years in prison.

The Federal Trade Commission

During 2010, the FTC continued to focus its law enforcement efforts on scams that target consumers hit hard by the economic downturn and on unemployment in particular. These efforts, done as coordinated initiatives with state and federal law enforcement partners, included the filing of 12 new FTC civil enforcement actions against operations that falsely claimed they could provide consumers with guaranteed jobs, the opportunity to earn substantial income from home, government grants or stimulus funds, or needed health care insurance.

By February 2011, four of these new actions had already been resolved. Seven prior actions against scammers who likewise sought to take advantage of consumers' vulnerability during the economic downtown were also recently resolved. The judgments in these matters total more than $80 million, a portion of which has been suspended because of the defendants' inability to pay. The following are two of the FTC's most significant recent matters:

◆ **Suit against 61 corporations and 10 individuals in massive Internet government grant and money making program scheme**

On December 22, 2010, the FTC filed suit against the 10 individuals and 61 corporations allegedly responsible for an Internet scheme that caused consumers to lose more than $275 million since its inception in 2006. According to the FTC's complaint, the enterprise, which operated under the name "I Works," tricked consumers into providing their credit and debit card information and repeatedly billed them for Internet-based memberships that they never agreed to join. The scheme lured consumers with allegedly false promises of government grants or money-making programs and, at its height, ensnared 15,000 consumers per day. To prevent the dissipation of assets during litigation, the FTC obtained a temporary restraining order, entered January 13, 2011, that freezes the assets of the alleged ringleader and the I Works corporate defendants.

- **Final order in Internet scheme involving false promises to consumers and surrender of $3 million to the FTC**

On October 4, 2010, the FTC obtained a stipulated final order dismantling a far-reaching Internet enterprise that operated under the names "Google Money Tree," "Google Treasure Chest," and similar variations. According to the FTC's complaint, the defendants used the name and logo of the Internet search company Google and false promises that consumers could earn $100,000 in six months to lure consumers into divulging their financial account information to pay a modest shipping fee for a work-at-home kit. The defendants allegedly failed to adequately disclose that buying the product would trigger automatic monthly charges of $72.21. Under the terms of the stipulated final order, the defendants have surrendered assets in excess of $3 million for redress to consumer victims. The order also bans the individuals behind the operation from ever again selling goods or services using "negative options"—that is, transactions in which the seller interprets consumers' silence or inaction as permission to charge them.

Financial Crimes Enforcement Network

In 2010, the Financial Crimes Enforcement Network (FinCEN) provided substantial financial intelligence and analysis to the law enforcement community. For example:

- FinCEN provided numerous securities fraud referrals to the SEC's Office of Market Intelligence. The SEC opened at least one new enforcement case based on the December 2010 hedge fund referral report to the Office of Market Intelligence, and has used the information in dozens of ongoing hedge fund cases.

- FinCEN initiated a case study using the Financial Industry Regulatory Authority (FINRA) data to identify reported suspicious activities of registered securities members who were barred from the industry. Strategic reports were published on suspicious activities with commercial mortgage backed securities (CMBS) in October 2010.

- FinCEN prepared a report for the SEC Asset Management Unit on hedge funds reported in SAR filings, which contained more than 320 hedge fund firms and $150 billion in suspicious activity.

- In February and March 2010, FinCEN provided research to the Iowa Attorney General's Office in support of a criminal case involving insider trading, market manipulation, check fraud and embezzlement. FinCEN identified $5 million in reported suspicious activities, as well as 11 related accounts and numerous associated shell companies.

- In July and August 2010, FinCEN provided support for a joint FBI and SEC case involving interstate transactions of an unregistered security, manipulative and deceptive devices, mail fraud and wire fraud. FinCEN identified $7 million in reported suspicious activities, 20 bank and credit union accounts and 3 casino accounts.

+ From March through October 2010, FinCEN provided support to the Florida Attorney General's Office in support of a criminal investigation of a Ponzi scheme. FinCEN identified $8 million in suspicious activities.

+ In November 2010, FinCEN supported an IRS-CI case involving hedge fund portfolio managers suspected of defrauding investors. FinCEN identified $85 million in reported suspicious activities, numerous hedge funds and associated individuals.

+ FinCEN identified 451 Bank Secrecy Act (BSA) reports on 241 barred members that indicated $382 million in suspicious financial activity, such as money laundering, forgery, market manipulation, hedge fund fraud, wire transfer fraud and embezzlement. A significant portion of this activity occurred after the members were barred from the securities industry.

Internal Revenue Service-Criminal Investigation

The IRS-CI fills a unique niche in the federal law enforcement community. Agents of IRS-CI conduct forensic financial probes and investigate corporations and their executives for tax fraud, money laundering and securities fraud. Its financial investigative expertise is necessarily called upon to unravel the complex myriad of investment fraud schemes perpetrated by defendants who prey on individuals. For IRS-CI, corporate securities fraud encompasses violations of the Internal Revenue Code (IRC) and related statutes committed by large, publicly traded or private corporations, and/or by their senior executives and their principal officers.

During 2010 IRS-CI has been involved in approximately 86 investigations that involved securities fraud.

+ **Petters Group Worldwide LLC**

In connection with the FBI's contributions to the SCFWG, IRS-CI also played a significant role in the ongoing investigation of this matter.

+ **Scott Rothstein**

In connection with the FBI's contributions to the SCFWG, IRS-CI also played a significant role in this matter.

+ **Trevor Cook**

In connection with the U.S. Attorney's Office for the District of Minnesota's contributions to the SCFWG, IRS-CI played a significant role in this matter.

The Securities and Exchange Commission

To help protect investors and maintain fair markets, the SEC brings enforcement actions against individuals and organizations for alleged violations of securities laws. Through the Division of Enforcement, the SEC stops fraud, seeks appropriate penalties and disgorgement from wrongdoers and returns funds to injured investors.

In 2010, the SEC filed 679 actions, which resulted in more than $3.26 billion in ordered disgorgement and penalties combined. The following is an outline of certain significant SEC enforcement cases in 2010. For further information on selected enforcement cases, please see "Litigation Releases" at *http://www.sec.gov/litigation/litreleases.shtml*.

Actions Related to the Financial Crisis

The SEC has continued to devote significant resources to identifying and holding accountable those firms and individuals who committed securities law violations linked to the financial crisis:

◆ In February 2010, the SEC charged **State Street Bank and Trust** with misleading investors about their exposure to subprime investments while selectively disclosing more complete information only to certain favored investors. The SEC alleged that State Street continued to market the fund as having better sector diversification than a typical money market fund, although the fund was almost entirely invested in subprime residential mortgage-backed securities and derivatives that magnified its exposure to subprime securities. To settle the SEC's action, State Street agreed to pay more than $300 million to investors who lost money during the subprime market meltdown in 2007.

◆ In April 2010, the SEC brought administrative proceedings against **Morgan Keegan & Company and Morgan Asset Management** and two employees, including a portfolio manager, for fraudulently overstating the value of securities backed by subprime mortgages. The SEC alleges that Morgan Keegan failed to employ reasonable procedures to internally price the portfolio securities in five funds managed by Morgan Asset, and consequently did not calculate accurate "net asset values" (NAV) for the funds. Morgan Keegan recklessly published these inaccurate daily NAVs, and sold shares to investors based on inflated prices. The misconduct masked the true impact of the subprime mortgage meltdown on these funds from investors. A hearing before an administrative law judge will be held.

◆ In another important action in April 2010, the SEC filed charges against **Goldman Sachs & Co.** and one of its employees, Fabrice Tourre, alleging fraud in connection with the marketing of a synthetic CDO, in which Goldman represented that the portfolio of securities underlying the CDO had been selected by a neutral, objective third party when, in reality, a hedge fund investor at whose request the CDO had been structured and whose interests were directly adverse to CDO investors, heavily influenced the portfolio selection. The Goldman marketing materials failed to disclose the hedge fund's role in the transaction, its adverse economic interests, or its role in the portfolio selection. On July 20, 2010, the court entered a consent judgment in which Goldman agreed to pay $550 million to settle the SEC's charges. The SEC's litigation continues against Fabrice Tourre.

◆ In June 2010, the SEC charged Lee B. Farkas, the former chairman of the once largest non-depository mortgage lender in the nation, **Taylor, Bean & Whitaker** (TBW), with allegedly orchestrating a large-scale securities fraud scheme and then attempting to defraud the U.S. Treasury's Troubled Asset Relief Program (TARP) to cover up the scheme. TBW sold more than $1.5 billion worth of fabricated or impaired mortgage loans and securities to Colonial Bank which were falsely reported to the investing public as high-quality, liquid assets. Farkas was also responsible for a bogus equity investment that caused Colonial BancGroup to misrepresent that it had satisfied a prerequisite necessary to qualify for TARP funds. The Treasury Department never awarded Colonial BancGroup any TARP funds. This case was the product of extensive cooperation with DOJ, FBI, SIGTARP, and other law enforcement partners within the Task Force.

- In July 2010, the SEC filed a settled action against **Citigroup Inc.** and two executives for misleading investors about the company's exposure to subprime mortgage-related assets. Between July and mid-October 2007, Citigroup represented during earnings calls and in public filings that subprime exposure in its investment banking unit was $13 billion or less, when in fact it was more than $50 billion. In the settlement, Citigroup agreed to pay a $75 million penalty and the executives agreed to injunctive relief and to pay $100,000 and $80,000 respectively.

- Later in July, the SEC accepted settlement offers from three former officers of **New Century Financial Corporation:** Brad A. Morrice, the former chief executive officer (CEO) and co-founder; Patti M. Dodge, the former chief financial officer (CFO); and David N. Kenneally, the former controller. The SEC's complaint alleged, among other things, that New Century's second and third quarter 2006 Forms 10-Q and two late 2006 private stock offerings contained false and misleading statements regarding its subprime mortgage business. The complaint further alleged that Morrice and Dodge knew about certain negative trends in New Century's loan portfolio from reports they received and that they participated in the disclosure process, but they did not take adequate steps to ensure that the negative trends were properly disclosed. The SEC's complaint also alleged that in the second and third quarters of 2006, Kenneally, contrary to Generally Accepted Accounting Principles, implemented changes to New Century's method for estimating its loan repurchase obligation and failed to ensure that New Century's backlog of pending loan repurchase requests were properly accounted for, resulting in an understatement of New Century's repurchase reserve and a material overstatement of New Century's financial results.

- In October 2010, the SEC announced that former **Countrywide Financial** CEO **Angelo Mozilo** would pay a record $22.5 million penalty to settle SEC charges that he and two other former Countrywide executives misled investors as the subprime mortgage crisis emerged. The settlement also permanently barred Mozilo from ever again serving as an officer or director of a publicly traded company. Mozilo's financial penalty is the largest ever paid by a public company's senior executive in an SEC settlement. Mozilo also agreed to $45 million in disgorgement of ill-gotten gains to settle the SEC's disclosure violation and insider trading charges against him, for a total financial settlement of $67.5 million, monies that are to be returned to harmed investors.

Actions Involving Offering Frauds/ Ponzi Schemes

Offering frauds comprise a significant portion of the cases brought by the SEC each year. Many offering frauds involved Ponzi schemes where investors are guaranteed unrealistic returns for their investment. In these actions, the SEC seeks where possible to freeze assets in order to maximize the recovery to investors and prevent new investors from being harmed.

In 2010, the SEC participated in *Operation Broken Trust,* a national investment fraud operation discussed further below. The SEC's enforcement efforts contributed 35 matters to the operation. The 35 SEC matters involved 130 defendants/respondents who caused approximately 20,804 investors an estimated $1.825 billion in losses. In addition:

- The SEC continued to vigorously pursue wrongdoers in the $50 billion Bernard Madoff Ponzi scheme. In February, the SEC charged **Daniel Bonventre,** Madoff's director of operations, with falsifying accounting records to enable the multi-billion dollar fraud to continue and to illegally enrich himself, Madoff and Madoff's family and employees. The complaint alleged that Bonventre played an essential role in the fraud by creating bogus financial records to give Bernard Madoff Investment Securities (BMIS) the appearance of legitimacy.

- In November 2010, the SEC obtained partial consent judgments permanently enjoining **Robert M. Jaffe, Maurice J. Cohn, Marcia B. Cohn** and **Cohmad Securities Corp**. The SEC's amended complaint alleges that these defendants referred hundreds of investors to Madoff and BMIS, while the defendants were aware of and failed to disclose facts that should have raised serious questions about the propriety of the Madoff investment. The investors referred to BMIS by the defendants provided BMIS with more than one billion dollars.

- Also in November 2010, the SEC charged **Annette Bongiorno** and **JoAnn Crupi**, two longtime employees of BMIS, with playing key roles in the Madoff Ponzi scheme. Among other things, the SEC complaint alleges that Bongiorno regularly created false books and records and helped mislead investors in telephone conversations and through account statements and trade confirmations that reported securities transactions that never happened and positions that never existed. Bongiorno also created false trades in her own BMIS accounts that enabled her to cash out millions of dollars more than she deposited. The SEC's complaint against Crupi alleges that she helped facilitate the fraud and mislead investors, auditors and regulators into believing that BMIS was a legitimate enterprise. When the fraud was on the verge of collapse, Crupi helped decide which accounts should be cashed out and prepared checks for those selected investors, many of whom were friends or family of Madoff. The SEC is litigating these actions and seeking dis-

gorgement and civil penalties. The SEC is continuing its investigation as to others.

Actions Involving Insider Trading

The SEC also brought numerous insider trading cases in 2010. Many of these cases involved Wall Street professionals and corporate insiders who undermined the level playing field that is fundamental to the fair functioning of the capital markets.

- In the **Galleon** matter, which the SEC initially charged in October 2009, the SEC continued to pursue and hold accountable those who participated in a massive insider trading scheme that generated more than $52 million in illegal profits or losses avoided. The SEC's initial complaint alleged that the billionaire Raj Rajaratnam paid bribes in exchange for inside information about corporate earnings or takeover activity and then used the non-public information to illegally trade on behalf of his New York-based hedge fund advisory firm Galleon Management LP. In related Galleon actions, the SEC charged 19 other high-ranking corporate executives and insiders involved in the insider trading scheme. During 2010, the SEC settled with four of the individual tippers and one of the entities involved. The SEC is seeking permanent injunctions, disgorgement and penalties in the remaining actions against Rajaratnam and others. The SEC's investigation is continuing.

- In late 2009, the SEC charged three Wall Street lawyers for tipping inside information in exchange for kickbacks and six Wall Street traders and a proprietary trading firm involved in a $20 million insider trading ring. In this action, the SEC alleged that two attorneys in the New York office of international law firm **Ropes & Gray** had access to confidential information about at least four major proposed corporate transactions in which the firm's clients participated. Through a friend and fellow attorney, these lawyers tipped this inside information to a proprietary trader at **Schottenfeld Group**. In 2010, the SEC filed two additional complaints naming three other defendants for conduct related to that described in the initial complaint and also settled with two defendants. Finally, the SEC filed in November 2010 two additional complaints for related conduct, one naming **Franz Tudor** as a defendant and a second complaint naming **Thomas Hardin** and **Lanexa Management LLC** as defendants. The litigation continues as to certain defendants.

- In August 2010, in an expedited investigation spearheaded by the Division of Enforcement's Market Abuse Unit, the SEC swiftly charged two residents of Madrid, Spain, with insider trading and obtained an emergency asset freeze. The residents made nearly $1.1 million by trading while in the possession of material non-public information in advance of a public announcement of a multi-billion dollar tender offer by BHP Billiton Plc to acquire **Potash Corp.** of Saskatchewan Inc. One of the defendants is the head of a research arm at Banco Santander S.A., a Spanish banking group advising BHP on its bid. In addition to the emergency relief, the SEC is seeking permanent injunctions, disgorgement and penalties. The SEC's investigation is continuing.

Municipal Bond Offerings and Pay-to-Play

In an investigation handled by the newly-created Municipal Securities and Public Pensions Unit, the SEC in August 2010 filed its first action ever against a state for violations of the federal securities laws. The SEC charged the **State of New Jersey** with securities fraud for misrepresenting and failing to disclose to investors billions of dollars of municipal bond offerings

that it was underfunding the state's two largest pension plans. New Jersey settled to a cease-and-desist order. In determining to accept this settlement, the SEC considered the cooperation afforded the SEC's staff during the investigation and certain remedial acts taken by the state. In addition:

- On October 28, 2010, U.S. District Judge Dana M. Sabraw approved a settlement between the SEC and four former **San Diego City** officials for their roles in misleading investors in municipal bonds about the city's fiscal problems related to its pension and retiree health care obligations. Former City Manager **Michael Uberuaga**, former Auditor & Comptroller **Edward Ryan**, former Deputy City Manager for Finance **Patricia Frazier**, and former City Treasurer **Mary Vattimo**, without admitting or denying the allegations, consented to the entry of final judgments that permanently enjoin them from future violations of certain federal securities law provisions. Under the settlement terms, Uberuaga, Ryan and Frazier each paid a penalty of $25,000 and Vattimo paid a penalty of $5,000. This marks the first time that the SEC secured financial penalties against city officials in a municipal bond fraud case.

- On November 18, 2010, the SEC charged former **Quadrangle Group** principal **Steven Rattner** with participating in a widespread kickback scheme to obtain investments from New York's largest pension fund. Rattner agreed to settle the SEC's charges by paying $6.2 million and consenting to a bar from associating with any investment adviser or broker-dealer for at least two years.

Separately, on April 15, 2010, Quadrangle Group LLC and Quadrangle GP Investors II L.P. consented to the entry of a judgment that permanently enjoins them from future violations of certain federal securities law provisions and ordered them to pay a $5 million penalty.

Actions Involving Issuer Disclosure and Reporting Violations

The SEC also brought numerous cases during 2010 involving financial fraud, issuer disclosure and reporting violations at public companies. For example:

- In July 2010, the SEC filed an action against **Dell Inc.,** for failing to supply accurate and complete information about the company's financial condition. The SEC also charged Dell chairman and CEO Michael Dell, former CEO Kevin Rollins and former CFO James Schneider for their roles in the disclosure violations. Additionally, the SEC charged Schneider, former regional vice president of finance Nicholas Dunning, and former assistant controller Leslie Jackson for their roles in the improper accounting. Dell agreed to pay a $100 million penalty to settle the SEC's charges; Michael Dell and Rollins each agreed to pay a $4 million penalty; and Schneider agreed to pay $3 million in disgorgement and penalties. Dunning and Jackson have also settled.

- In March 2010, the SEC charged three former senior executives and a former director of an Omaha-based database compilation company, **infoUSA Inc.,** for their roles in a scheme in which the former CEO and Chairman, Vinod Gupta, fraudulently used corporate funds to pay almost $9.5 million in personal expenses to support his lavish lifestyle. Additionally, Gupta caused the company to enter into $9.3 million of undisclosed related party transactions with Gupta's other entities. The SEC also alleged that the former chairman of the audit committee, Vasant Raval, failed to respond appropriately to various red flags concerning Gupta's expenses and related party transactions. Further,

two of the company's former chief financial officers rubber-stamped hundreds of Gupta's reimbursement requests despite the fact that the requests lacked sufficient explanation of business purpose and supporting documentation. Gupta settled this action and agreed to pay more than $7.4 million in disgorgement and to an officer and director bar. Raval agreed to settle this action and to a $50,000 penalty and an officer and director bar. The action against the two former CFOs is in litigation. In a related administrative proceeding, infoUSA consented to a cease-and-desist order.

- In January 2010, the SEC brought an action against **General Re Corporation** for its involvement in separate schemes by AIG and Prudential Financial to manipulate and falsify their reported financial results. Gen Re arranged to sell financial products to AIG and Prudential for the sole purpose of enabling those companies to manipulate their accounting results and mislead investors. Gen Re agreed to settle with the SEC and pay $12.2 million in disgorgement and prejudgment interest.

The U.S. Attorneys' Offices

U.S. Attorney's Office for the District of Colorado

- **Philip R. Lochmiller and Phillip R. Lochmiller II**

Owners and operators of Valley Investments, Philip R. Lochmiller of Mack, Colorado, and Philip R. Lochmiller II presently of Olathe, Kansas, as well as a Valley Investments employee, Shawnee N. Carver of Grand Junction, Colorado, were indicted by a federal grand jury in Denver on December 15, 2009, on conspiracy and fraud charges. Between 2000 and 2009, Lochmiller and Lochmiller II caused Valley Investments to receive approximately $31 million from approximately 400 investors as part of the securities and mail fraud scheme charged in the indictment. Lochmiller II and Carver both entered guilty pleas in 2010 and are scheduled for sentencing after trial of Philip Lochmiller, which will take place in July 2011. This case was investigated by the FBI, IRS-CI and USPIS, with substantial assistance from the State of Colorado Division of Securities and the Mesa County Sheriff's Office.

U.S. Attorney's Office for the Southern District of Illinois

◆ Nicholas Smirnow

Nicholas A. Smirnow, formerly of Ontario, Canada, was charged on May 28, 2010, in a criminal complaint in the Southern District of Illinois with various counts of conspiracy, mail fraud, wire fraud and securities fraud in connection with an international high yield investment and Ponzi scheme that resulted in losses of $70 million to more than 40,000 investors in more than 120 countries in six continents. The scheme operated from Canada and the Philippines, through a website hosted in the Netherlands, and through a company supposedly based in the Turks & Caicos Islands in the Caribbean. Smirnow called his investment scam "Pathway to Prosperity" and he used his Internet website to snare investors. The Pathway to Prosperity website claimed that investors could earn extremely high rates of returns with minimal or no risk in 7, 15, 30 and 60-day "plans." While some earlier investors received a substantial return on their investment, most investors lost everything. The complaint alleges that Pathway to Prosperity made few, if any, legitimate investments. The case was investigated by the USPIS-Chicago Division, with substantial assistance from the IRS and the Ontario Provincial Police in Canada. Assistance was also provided by the Rotterdam-Rijnmond Regional Police in the Netherlands and the Illinois Securities Department.

U.S. Attorney's Office for the District of Minnesota

◆ Petters Group Worldwide LLC

As explained above in connection with the FBI's contributions to the SCFWG, in April 2010, the U.S. Attorney's Office for Minnesota secured a 50-year prison term in the case against Petters, one of the longest financial crimes-related sentences. In addition, five other individual conspirators were sentenced to prison in 2010. The U.S. Attorney's Office, working with the FBI, the IRS-CI, and USPIS, is continuing its investigation into the Petters ponzi scheme and several PCI hedge fund investors.

◆ Trevor Cook

In August 2010, Trevor Cook was sentenced to 25 years in prison for orchestrating a Ponzi scheme that collectively cost more than 900 investors $158 million. Cook, of Apple Valley, Minnesota, was charged with and pleaded guilty to one count of mail fraud and one count of tax evasion in connection with his crime. In imposing the sentence, U.S. District Court Judge James M. Rosenbaum described Cook's offense as "wretched, tawdry, and cheap." In his plea agreement, Cook admitted that from January 2007 through July 2009, he carried out a scheme to defraud people by purportedly selling investments in a foreign currency trading program. In reality, however, he diverted a substantial portion of the money provided him for other purposes, including making payments to previous investors; providing funds to Crown Forex SA, in an effort to deceive Swiss banking regulators; purchasing ownership interest in two trading firms; buying a real estate development in Panama; paying personal expenses, including gambling debts; and acquiring a well-known mansion in Minneapolis.

✦ Gregory Malcolm Bell

Gregory Malcolm Bell was sentenced on September 30, 2010, to six years in prison on one count of wire fraud. Bell's hedge fund, Lancelot Investment Management, had almost all its money invested in Petters Company Inc. (PCI) promissory notes. When PCI fell behind in its payments on those notes, Bell devised a plan to make it appear to his investors that PCI was still paying on time. The result was 86 sham "round trip" transactions, where Lancelot gave money to PCI, which PCI then used to make payments back to Lancelot. As a result of the scheme, Bell was able to raise more than $200 million from 43 new investors during 2008.

U.S. Attorney's Office for the District of New Jersey

✦ Nevin Shapiro

The former owner and chief executive officer of Capitol Investments USA Inc., Nevin Shapiro, pleaded guilty on September 15, 2010, in the District of New Jersey, for his role in a multi-million dollar investment fraud scheme. From January 2005 through November 2009, Shapiro solicited investors from New Jersey and throughout the United States through Capitol, telling them that he would use their money to fund his wholesale grocery distribution business. As a result of these solicitations, investors sent more than $880 million to Shapiro and Capitol during this time period. Capitol had virtually no income generating business at that time and Shapiro used new investor funds to make principal and interest payments to existing investors, as well as to fund his own lavish lifestyle. Shapiro used investor funds to pay illegal sports gambling debts, to purchase floor seats at Miami Heat basketball games and to make payments on his Riviera yacht and his residence in

Miami Beach. Shapiro also used investor funds to make payments to student athletes attending a local university in the Miami area and to make donations to the university. The fraud scheme resulted in an estimated loss of $89 million to 75 victims. The case was investigated by the FBI and IRS-CI, with coordination from the SEC, which previously had filed parallel civil charges.

U.S. Attorney's Office for the Eastern District of New York

✦ Philip Barry

On November 17, 2010, investment manager Philip Barry was convicted at trial of one count of securities fraud and 33 counts of mail fraud in connection with his operation of a long-standing and large-scale Ponzi scheme. Approximately 800 individuals invested a total of more than $40 million in Barry's business, the Leverage Group. To induce investments and discourage withdrawals, Barry, among other things, guaranteed specified positive rates of return, issued account statements that showed growing account balances, represented that investing in the Leverage Group was safe and promised that withdrawals could be made easily. The evidence at trial established that Barry actually was running a Ponzi scheme, paying returns to Leverage Group investors not from any profits earned on investments, but rather from existing investors' deposits or money paid by new investors. Barry never produced or earned the rates of return that he advertised and cited in clients' account statements. Rather, the positive rates of return were simply pre-determined interest rates made up by Barry. In bankruptcy testimony given by Barry, he estimated that he owed his investors $60 million. In bankruptcy proceedings, the U.S. Trustee Program secured from Barry a waiver of chapter 7 discharge.

U.S. Attorney's Office for the Southern District of New York

✦ Insider Trading Cases

In 2010, the U.S. Attorney's Office in the Southern District of New York (USAO SDNY) continued its successful prosecutions of insider trading crimes, filing charges against 15 individuals, nine of whom have since pleaded guilty. Also in 2010, the USAO secured guilty pleas from six individuals who were charged with insider trading crimes in late 2009. Among those who pleaded guilty in 2010 were co-conspirators of Raj Rajaratnam, who served as the managing member of Galleon Management LLC, and as a portfolio manager for Galleon Technology Offshore Ltd. Rajaratnam was charged for insider trading crimes in late 2009 and in May 2011, he was convicted on securities fraud charges.

In January 2010, Anil Kumar, formerly a senior partner and director at the global management consulting firm McKinsey & Company, pleaded guilty to conspiring to commit insider trading crimes with Rajaratnam. Rajiv Goel, a former executive at Intel Corp., pleaded guilty in February 2010 to conspiracy and securities fraud charges stemming from his involvement in an insider trading scheme with Rajaratnam.

Mark Kurland, a senior managing director at New Castle Partners; Ali Hariri, formerly an executive at Atheros Communications Inc.; Robert Moffat Jr., a former executive with IBM; and David Plate, formerly a proprietary trader at Schottenfeld Group LLC, each pleaded guilty in 2010 to separate charges related to insider trading schemes.

In November 2010, Don Ching Trang Chu, a/k/a "Don Chu," was arrested on conspiracy charges in connection with his employment at an expert networking firm. Chu was charged with conspiring to promote the firm's consultation services by arranging for insiders at publicly-traded companies to provide material, nonpublic information to the firm's hedge fund clients for the purpose of executing profitable securities transactions. In December 2010, James Fleishman, an executive for an expert-networking firm, was charged in a complaint with wire fraud and conspiracy charges for conspiring to provide confidential information, including material, nonpublic information, to the firm's clients, including hedge funds. Mark Anthony Longoria, Walter Shimoon and Manosha Karunatilaka were charged with the same offenses in the same complaint in connection with their employment as consultants for the firm.

Daniel DeVore, formerly a Global Supply Manager for Dell Inc., who worked as a consultant for an expert-networking firm, pleaded guilty in December 2010 to an information charging him with wire fraud and conspiracy to commit wire fraud and securities fraud in connection with his work as a consultant. Also in December 2010, Winifred Jiau, a/k/a "Wini," was charged in a complaint for her involvement in an insider trading scheme. Jiau was charged with conspiring to commit securities fraud and engaging in securities fraud, by selling material, nonpublic information about publicly traded companies to multiple hedge funds for the purpose of executing profitable securities transactions.

Joseph Contorinis, a former hedge fund manager, was found guilty at trial in October 2010 for his participation in a scheme to trade on inside information obtained from a former UBS banker that resulted in more than $7 million in illegal profits. Contorinis was subsequently sentenced to six years in prison.

In November 2010, Yves Benhamou, a citizen and resident of France, was charged in a complaint with engaging in an insider trading scheme in which he used his dual roles as an adviser on a clinical drug trial and as a private, paid consultant to provide material, nonpublic information about the drug trial's progress to a portfolio manager of a hedge fund group. Igor Poteroba, a former investment banker in the Healthcare Group of UBS Securities LLC, and Alexei P. Koval, a/k/a "Aleksey Koval," were arrested in March 2010 on charges relating to their participation in an insider trading scheme in which Poteroba obtained inside information about six mergers and acquisitions that certain UBS clients were contemplating and then passed that information to Koval.

◆ Investment Frauds

In 2010, the USAO SDNY continued to investigate and prosecute matters related to the Bernard Madoff Ponzi scheme. In November 2010, Daniel Bonventre, Annette Bongiorno, Joann Crupi, Jerome O'Hara and George Perez, all former employees of Bernard L. Madoff Investment Securities LLC (BLMIS), were charged in a superseding indictment with, among other crimes, conspiracy, falsifying records of a broker-dealer and falsifying records of an investment adviser. Civil forfeiture complaints were filed against more than $7 million in assets belonging to former BLMIS employees Annette Bongiorno and Joann Crupi.

In December 2010, Carl J. Shapiro and various related people and entities agreed to forfeit $625 million to the United States, all of which will be made available to the victims of Bernard L. Madoff and BLMIS.

The estate of Jeffry M. Picower agreed in December 2010 to forfeit $7,206,157,717 to the United States, representing all the profits that Picower withdrew from BLMIS, the fraudulent investment advisory business owned and operated by Bernard L. Madoff.

In addition to the Madoff scam, the USAO SDNY also prosecuted significant investment fraud matters.

Vance Moore II and Walter Netschi were charged with operating a fraud scheme involving the sale of investments in automated teller machines (ATMs) that would purportedly be placed in retail locations around the country. The defendants successfully solicited more than $80 million in investments. In fact, approximately 90 percent of the machines purportedly sold to the victims did not exist or were not owned by the defendants. Moore pleaded guilty in October 2010, just prior to trial, and Netschi was convicted in November 2010.

U.S. Attorney's Office for the Western District of North Carolina

◆ Keith Franklin Simmons

On December 16, 2010, Keith Franklin Simmons was convicted at trial on all counts of securities fraud, wire fraud and money laundering relating to his leadership of a $40 million forex fraud scheme. Simmons was the owner of Black Diamond Capital Solutions and claimed to have access to a secret foreign currency exchange trading platform. The scheme took in more than $40 million from more than 400 investors around the country, many of whom invested their life savings. Prior to Simmons' trial, four other defendants — Deanna Salazar, James Jordan, Steven Lacy and Roy Scarboro — pleaded guilty to their involvement in the Black Diamond scheme, admitting that although Simmons told them his investments were legitimate, they each deceived investors themselves in some way. The case was investigated by the FBI and IRS-CI.

◆ Terry Welch

Terry Scott Welch was a vice president at Wachovia Bank and pleaded guilty to an $11 million conspiracy to defraud Wachovia. Welch directed four co-conspirators John Cousar, Delmar Dove, Jerry Little and Robert Otto, all of whom also pleaded guilty to transmit false invoices through their respective businesses to

Wachovia. Thereafter, Welch caused Wachovia to issue payment for the invoices totaling more than $11 million during the nearly eight-year time period of the conspiracy. In addition, Welch, Cousar and Dove pleaded guilty to tax charges arising from the scheme. The case was investigated by the USPIS, IRS-CI, and the North Carolina State Bureau of Investigation.

◆ Bryan Noel

Bryan Noel was convicted in March 2010 and later sentenced to 25 years in prison for leading an investment fraud that took more than $10 million from more than 100 victims, most of whom were retirees. His co-conspirator, Alex Klosek, received 87 months in prison. Noel diverted more than $4 million of the retirees' funds to his risky start-up companies, including a mineral exploration venture in Peru and a composite lumber company, both of which failed. Investors were not told of these diversions. The case was investigated by the FBI and North Carolina Secretary of State's Office, Securities Division.

U.S. Attorney's Office for the Eastern District of Pennsylvania

◆ Robert Stinson

Robert Stinson Jr. was charged in 2010 with mail and wire fraud, money laundering and filing false tax returns for his participation in a Ponzi scheme that caused more than $17 million in losses. Stinson claimed to operate several hedge funds known as "Life's Good" and sought investments from individuals with IRAs and claimed that he would make investments in real estate and obtain security for the loans. He told prospective investors that their investments posed very little risk because of the security. Instead of investing the money, Stinson allegedly used it to pay his personal and other expenses.

Stinson bilked hundreds of investors. The case was investigated by the FBI, USPIS and IRS-CI.

U.S. Attorney's Office for the Eastern District of Texas

◆ Joseph Blimline

Joseph Blimline pleaded guilty in the Eastern District of Texas on August 31, 2010, for his role in one of North Texas' largest oil and gas investment fraud schemes, which defrauded 7,700 investors of more than $485 million. Blimline was a majority owner of Provident Royalties, an investment company. Beginning in 2006, Blimline and others involved at Provident Royalties made false representations and failed to disclose other material facts to their investors to induce the investors into providing payments to Provident. The investors were not told that Blimline had received millions of dollars of unsecured loans and had been previously charged with securities fraud. Blimline issued approximately 20 oil and gas offerings, and used a significant amount of the money raised in these offerings to purchase oil and gas assets from earlier offerings and to pay dividends to earlier investors in order to facilitate the scheme. Blimline also pleaded guilty to charges related to a separate, but similar oil and gas scheme based in Michigan that defrauded investors out of $50 million. The criminal case against Blimline was investigated by the FBI, in coordination with the SEC, which previously had filed a civil action to freeze the assets of Blimline and others.

U.S. Postal Inspection Service

USPIS investigated a host of significant enforcement efforts in 2010, including, but not limited to, these cases discussed above: the case against David Lewalski for an alleged $30 million investment fraud scheme; the prosecution of seven individuals for their alleged roles in the

A&O investment fraud scheme; and the prosecution of George David Gordon and Richard Clark for a $43 million pump-and-dump stock manipulation scheme.

Operation Broken Trust

Several actions discussed above were a part of Operation Broken Trust. Operation Broken Trust was a nationwide Task Force operation targeting investment fraud. The operation involved enforcement actions against 310 criminal defendants and 189 civil defendants for fraud schemes that harmed more than 120,000 victims throughout the country.

The operation was conducted in conjunction with the SCFWG including with various Department of Justice components — the U.S. Attorneys' Offices, the FBI, the Criminal and Civil Divisions and the U.S. Trustee Program — as well as the SEC, USPIS, the CFTC, IRS-CI, the FTC, the U.S. Secret Service and the National Association of Attorneys General.

The operation's criminal cases involved more than $8 billion in estimated losses and the civil cases involved estimated losses of more than $2 billion. Operation Broken Trust was the first national operation of its kind to focus on a broad array of investment fraud schemes that directly preyed upon the investing public.

A LOOK AHEAD

The SCFWG will continue to meet, share ideas, and pursue robust fraud enforcement in 2011. Each of the working group's members remains committed to continuing the strong partnerships that the group has developed, and to aggressively investigating and prosecuting securities and commodities fraud in the coming year.

Non-Discrimination Working Group

INTRODUCTION

The Non-Discrimination Working Group of the Task Force is chaired by Thomas Perez, Assistant Attorney General for the Civil Rights Division of the Justice Department; Michelle Aronowitz, Deputy General Counsel for Enforcement and Fair Housing of the Department of Housing and Urban Development (HUD); Sandy Braunstein, Director of the Division of Consumer and Community Affairs of the Federal Reserve Board; and the National Association of Attorneys General, represented by Attorney General Lisa Madigan of Illinois.

The Non-Discrimination Working Group focuses on financial fraud and other unfair practices directed at people or neighborhoods based on race, color, religion, national origin, sex, age, disability or any other basis prohibited by law. These practices — which can include charging minorities higher prices for credit, providing less favorable financial services to minority neighborhoods and steering minorities to more expensive loan products — create an unlevel playing field and have no place in our country. Through innovative federal interagency cooperation and state-federal partnerships, the Non-Discrimination Working Group is rooting out these illegal discriminatory practices. The Non-Discrimination Working Group is monitoring new practices and trends that have emerged since the subprime crisis to address proactively any emerging discriminatory practices.

Working group members include federal agencies with responsibility for enforcing laws that prohibit discrimination in lending and state law enforcement agencies.

- Civil Rights Division, Department of Justice (DOJ)(co-chair): Through the Civil Rights Division, the DOJ has responsibility for federal court enforcement of the Fair Housing Act, 42 U.S.C. § 3601, the Equal Credit Opportunity Act (ECOA), 15 U.S.C. § 1691, and the Servicemembers Civil Relief Act, 50 App. U.S.C. § 501. Other Justice Department components who are members of the working group are the Civil Division, the Criminal Division, the FBI and the Executive Office for U.S. Attorneys, representing the U.S. Attorneys.

- HUD (co-chair): HUD's Office of Fair Housing and Equal Opportunity (FHEO) is responsible for investigating Fair Housing Act complaints, issuing regulations under the statute, and providing grants to organizations, as well as state and local governments, to engage in fair housing enforcement and educational activities. HUD's Office of General Counsel represents HUD in administrative enforcement actions under the Act. HUD, through the Federal Housing Administration's (FHA) Mortgagee Review Board, oversees FHA-approved lenders' compliance with FHA program requirements and federal law, including anti-discrimination law.

- The Federal Reserve Board (co-chair): The Board ensures that the institutions it supervises comply fully with the federal fair lending laws—ECOA and the Fair Housing Act.

- The Office of the Illinois Attorney General (co-chair): The Office of the Illinois Attorney General is responsible for protecting the public interest and acting on behalf of the people of Illinois victimized by discriminatory, fraudu-

lent, deceptive and unfair business practices. Law enforcement actions are taken by the Attorney General to enforce state civil rights and consumer protection laws. The Office of the Illinois Attorney General represents the state attorney general community on the working group.

- Other members of the working group include the Federal Trade Commission (FTC), the Treasury Department, the Special Inspector General for the Troubled Asset Relief Program, and federal bank regulatory agencies, including the Federal Deposit Insurance Corporation (FDIC), the National Credit Union Administration (NCUA) and the Office of the Comptroller of the Currency (OCC).

FAIR LENDING: A FEDERAL GOVERNMENT PRIORITY

In 2010, there was an increase in resources devoted to fair lending enforcement across the federal government. This led to stepped up enforcement and an increase in the number of investigations that are expected to yield cases in the coming year. In 2010, the bank regulatory agencies and HUD combined referred more matters involving a potential pattern or practice of discrimination to the Department of Justice than in any year in at least the last 20 years. The bank regulators and HUD referred 49 matters to the Justice Department, 26 of which involved possible discrimination on the basis of race or national origin. This is a marked increase over the previous year's total of 11 referrals involving possible discrimination based on race or national origin.

The most common claim in fair lending enforcement actions brought during 2010 involved pricing discrimination, which is charging borrowers more because of their race or national origin than similarly qualified white applicants. The pricing discrimination cases involved loans made in the subprime market prior to 2007, as well as lenders active in the current mortgage market. Enforcement actions brought by the Office of the Illinois Attorney General involved allegations that lenders steered borrowers to more expensive loans because of borrowers' race or national origin. In addition, in 2010 HUD resolved a complaint involving allegations that a bank failed to serve minority neighborhoods.

OUTREACH AND INITIATIVES

The Non-Discrimination Working Group held three outreach events in 2010:

◆ **Chicago:** On April 22, 2010, the working group hosted the Non-Discrimination Working Group's Fair Lending Forum at the Federal Reserve Bank of Chicago. The purpose of the Forum was for the working group to hear from Illinois housing organizations and community groups concerning fair lending issues. Panelists included researchers, representatives of community-based organizations and housing counselors. After the Forum, members of the Non-Discrimination Working Group went on a tour of Chicago's Back of the Yards Neighborhood that was organized with the assistance of Neighborhood Housing Services of Chicago. The tour of the neighborhood included visiting various blocks that were devastated by subprime lending and mortgage fraud.

◆ **Washington, D.C.:** On June 14, 2010, the working group hosted the Non-Discrimination working group's roundtable discussion on non-discrimination in mortgage servicing and loan modifications at HUD. Roundtable participants included housing counselors, state regulators, homeowner's advocates and civil rights organizations.

◆ **Washington, D.C.:** On July 30, 2010, the working group hosted the Non-Discrimination working group's second roundtable discussion on non-discrimination in mortgage servicing and loan modifications at DOJ. Roundtable participants included mortgage servicers, lenders and other industry representatives.

In addition to the working group events, working group members conducted a significant amount of outreach to the general public and industry representatives. For example:

◆ Working group members spoke at dozens of conferences across the country to discuss fair lending enforcement priorities at the federal and state level.

◆ HUD continued its national education and outreach media campaign, which began in 2009, to address three major areas: (1) Foreclosure Prevention, (2) Predatory Lending Prevention, and (3) Rental Discrimination. HUD, in cooperation with the Treasury Department, has linked this national education and outreach campaign to Treasury's Makinghomeaffordable.gov website. The campaign has received more than $10 million in donated media and resulted in more than 600 million audience "impressions" through 2009 and 2010.

◆ In July 2010, HUD hosted a National Fair Housing Policy Conference in New Orleans. On July 22, 2010, the conference devoted a full morning to fair lending. Breakout sessions included: (1) How to Investigate a Fair Lending Case; (2) Home Mortgage Disclosure Act (HMDA) and FHA Loan Data; and (3) Loan Modification Programs Discrimination. More than 1,000 people, including state and local fair housing agencies and private fair housing groups, attended the policy conference.

- The FTC distributed more than 22,000 copies of its consumer education publication, "Mortgage Discrimination: A Guide to Understanding Your Rights & Taking Action," published in both English and Spanish, during 2010.

- On November 16, 2010, the FDIC hosted a Fair Lending Teleconference open to the banking industry which discussed how the FDIC reviews institutions flagged for disparities based on analysis of HMDA data and identifies areas of fair lending risk within their institutions' programs and processes. More than 3,000 representatives from the banking industry registered for this event. Questions received from this event were posted with answers on the FDIC's website. Similarly, bankers' calls also took place at regional offices where bankers in that region were invited to call in.

- On November 17, 2010, the Federal Reserve System held a webinar that provided information to the banking industry on how to correctly report HMDA and Community Reinvestment Act (CRA) data. HMDA and CRA data are critical to fair lending enforcement efforts because they can be used to identify illegal practices including pricing discrimination and redlining. The webinar also provided information on how banks can use HMDA and CRA data to monitor their own compliance with fair lending laws. More than 3,000 representatives of the banking industry participated in the webinar.

The membership of the working group has been proactive in finding ways to target discriminatory conduct in key market segments:

- ***Fair Lending and Loan Modification Initiative:*** The Non-Discrimination Working Group is particularly concerned that homeowners receive fair treatment from lenders and others offering to assist borrowers at risk of foreclosure. The working group is focused on ensuring that loan modification programs are administrated in a fair and non-discriminatory manner. HUD used its authority under the Fair Housing Act to require that all loan servicers participating in the federal government's Home Affordable Modification Program (HAMP) collect and report data on the race, ethnicity and sex of HAMP borrowers. Under the leadership of the Federal Reserve, a subcommittee of the working group is collaborating on analysis of the HAMP race and ethnicity data.

- ***FHA Loan Initiative:*** The working group has placed a special emphasis on ensuring that FHA-insured loans are available to all qualified borrowers on a non-discriminatory basis. In the wake of the collapse of the mortgage market, the number of FHA-insured loans has increased dramatically. HUD, together with DOJ and the Federal Reserve, has developed fair lending screens to examine FHA loan data and identify disparities that may warrant investigation. Using the results from this screening, HUD and DOJ have initiated several investigations. In addition, DOJ reached a settlement with Prime-Lending, based on a referral by the Federal Reserve, which resolved allegations of pricing discrimination, including discrimination in the pricing of FHA-insured mortgages.

- ***Fair Lending Initiative:*** Through the Patricia Roberts Harris National Fair Housing Training Academy, HUD has conducted a Fair Lending Initiative to combat the effects of the mortgage lending crisis. The courses, entitled "Buyer Beware," "Preventing Foreclosure," "Financial Aspects of Lending" and "Predatory Lending," are geared toward housing providers, housing counselors and homeowners. The courses emphasize teaching consumers how to identify and avoid deceptive mortgage lending practices.

- *Rulemaking on Equal Access to Housing in HUD Programs — Regardless of Sexual Orientation or Gender Identity:* HUD published a proposed rule in the Federal Register on January 24, 2011. Among the protections for lesbian, gay, bisexual and transgender persons set out in the proposed rule are provisions intended to ensure that sexual orientation and gender identity are not grounds for decision-making in FHA programs. The proposed rule specifies that determinations of adequacy of mortgagor income shall be made in a uniform manner without regard to actual or perceived sexual orientation or gender identity of the mortgagor.

TRAINING AND COORDINATION

- The FDIC, Federal Reserve, OCC, DOJ and HUD held internal trainings for their attorneys, investigators and examiners on fair lending. Several of these trainings included material presented by other working group members.

SIGNIFICANT ENFORCEMENT ACTIONS

Department of Housing and Urban Development

- *EHOC v. First National Bank of St. Louis.* In December 2010, HUD FHEO, the Metropolitan St. Louis Equal Housing Opportunity Council (EHOC), and First National Bank of St. Louis and Central Bancompany reached an agreement that will increase the bank's commitment to minority and low-income communities. As part of the agreement, the bank will invest more than $2.5 million over four years in St. Louis City,

Missouri; North St. Louis County, Missouri; and St. Clair County, Illinois. The agreement resulted from FHEO investigating and conciliating a fair housing complaint that was filed by EHOC, a fair housing organization, which alleged that the bank failed to locate branches and provide banking services in African-American neighborhoods.

- HUD obtained a settlement with an FHA-approved lender of allegations that it had failed to file mortgage data as required under the HMDA. Under the settlement, DAS Acquisition Company LLC, agreed to pay a $100,000 civil money penalty and accept a Letter of Reprimand from the Mortgagee Review Board.

- HUD and its fair housing assistance partners, including state and local agencies certified by HUD to enforce the Fair Housing Act, conciliated 102 lending discrimination cases in 2010 and helped recover more than $1.24 million in compensation.

Department of Justice

- On March 4, 2010, the United States filed a fair lending complaint and consent order resolving *United States v. AIG Federal Savings Bank and Wilmington Finance Inc.* AIG Federal Savings Bank (FSB) and Wilmington Finance Inc. (WFI), two subsidiaries of American International Group Inc., have agreed to pay a minimum of $6.1 million to resolve allegations that they engaged in a pattern or practice of discrimination against African American borrowers. This case resulted from a referral by the Treasury Department's Office of Thrift Supervision to the Justice Department's Civil Rights Division. The complaint alleges that the two defendants violated the Fair Housing Act and ECOA when they charged higher fees on thousands of subprime wholesale loans to African American borrowers nationwide from July 2003 until May 2006, a period of time before the federal government obtained an ownership interest in American International Group Inc. Under the settlement, AIG FSB and WFI will pay up to $6.1 million to African American customers who were charged higher broker fees than non-Hispanic white customers and will invest at least $1 million in consumer financial education.

◆ On December 9, 2010, the United States filed a fair lending complaint and proposed consent order resolving *United States v. PrimeLending*. This case resulted from a referral by the Federal Reserve Board to the Justice Department's Civil Rights Division in 2009. The complaint alleged that the defendant engaged in a pattern or practice of discrimination against African American borrowers nationwide between 2006 and 2009. The defendant, a national mortgage lender with 168 offices in 32 states became, in 2009, one of the nation's 20 largest FHA lenders. PrimeLending did not have monitoring in place to ensure that it complied with the fair lending laws, even as it grew to originate more than $5.5 billion in loans per year. The consent order requires the defendants to pay $2 million to the victims of discrimination and put in place loan pricing policies, monitoring and employee training that ensure discrimination does not occur in the future. The complaint alleges that the defendant violated the Fair Housing Act and the Equal Credit Opportunity Act when it charged African-American borrowers higher annual percentage rates of interest between 2006 and 2009 for prime fixed-rate home loans and for home loans guaranteed by the FHA and Department of Veterans Affairs than it charged to similarly-situated white borrowers. Prime-Lending's policy of giving its employees wide discretion to increase their commissions by adding overages to loans, which increased the interest rates paid by borrowers, had a disparate impact on African-American borrowers.

Federal Trade Commission

◆ In September 2010, the FTC reached a major settlement in its disparate impact litigation against Golden Empire Mortgage and its owner. The FTC alleged that the defendants violated the ECOA by charging Hispanic consumers higher prices for mortgage loans than non-Hispanic white consumers, disparities that could not be explained by the applicant's credit or risk characteristics. The price disparities resulted from the defendants' discretionary pricing policy that allowed loan officers and branch managers wide discretion to charge some borrowers "overages," *i.e.*, higher interest rates and up-front charges than the risk-based price of the loan. The order imposed a $5.5 million judgment, all but $1.5 million of which is suspended based on the defendants' financial situation. The money is being used to provide redress to about 3,200 consumers who were harmed by the defendants' pricing policy. Additionally, the settlement imposed obligations on the defendants to limit discretionary pricing, implement a fair lending monitoring program, conduct employee fair lending training, ensure data integrity and conduct regular compliance reporting.

◆ In January 2010, the FTC entered into a modified settlement with Gateway Funding Diversified Mortgage Services L.P. and its general partner, Gateway Funding Inc. The FTC alleged that Gateway failed to create its own effective fair-lending monitoring program, despite its agreement to do so in a December 2008 settlement of FTC charges of ECOA violations. The modified order requires Gateway to hire a third-party consultant to assist it in developing this fair lending compliance and monitoring program. The agreement also limits Gateway's discretion over pricing until the consultant certifies that an adequate monitoring program is in place. Previously, in

December 2008, the FTC reached a settlement with Gateway to resolve allegations that Gateway violated ECOA by charging African-American and Hispanic consumers higher prices for mortgage loans than non-Hispanic white consumers. The settlement imposed a judgment of $2.9 million, all but $200,000 of which was suspended based on inability to pay. The FTC used this money to redress about 2,000 African-American and Hispanic consumers who were harmed by Gateway's practices.

Office of the Illinois Attorney General

♦ On June 29, 2010, the Office of the Illinois Attorney General Lisa Madigan filed suit against Countrywide Home Loans Inc., Countrywide Financial Corporation and Full Spectrum Lending Inc. for steering prime-eligible African American and Latino borrowers into subprime mortgages and for charging African American and Latino borrowers more for certain mortgage products from 2005 through 2007 in Illinois. The Illinois Attorney General's complaint alleges that Countrywide's discretionary product selection and pricing policy allowed employees and brokers to alter terms, conditions or privileges of real estate transactions resulting in the steering of prime-eligible African American and Latino borrowers into subprime mortgages and in giving African American and Latino borrowers mortgages that are costlier than mortgages given to similarly-situated white borrowers in violation of the Illinois Human Rights Act. The Illinois Attorney General's complaint also alleges that Countrywide's discretionary product selection and pricing policy had an adverse and disparate impact on African American and Latino borrowers in Illinois, as compared to similarly-situated white borrowers in violation of the Illinois Human Rights Act. The complaint also alleges that Countrywide utilized lending standards that have no economic basis and are discriminatory in effect, in violation of the Illinois Fairness in Lending Act. The Illinois Attorney General is seeking restitution for all of the victims and civil penalties of $25,000 per violation of the Illinois Human Rights Act.

♦ In addition, the Illinois Attorney General's litigation against Wells Fargo and Company, Wells Fargo Bank N.A., also doing business as Wells Fargo Home Mortgage, and Wells Fargo Financial Illinois Inc., which was filed on July 31, 2009, is ongoing. The Illinois Attorney General's complaint alleges that Wells Fargo steered prime-eligible African American and Latino borrowers into subprime mortgages.

Federal Deposit Insurance Corporation

In 2010, the FDIC issued civil money penalties in three fair lending cases. Each of these cases had been referred to the Department of Justice but returned to the FDIC for administrative enforcement action.

♦ **EvaBank** — The FDIC cited the bank for violating ECOA and the Fair Housing Act after finding that the bank engaged in a pattern or practice of discrimination in 2005 when, for certain residential mortgage loans, the bank charged higher interest rates to Hispanic borrowers than it charged to other similarly situated non-Hispanic white borrowers. The bank was assessed a $15,000 civil money penalty.

♦ **Merchants and Planters Bank** — The FDIC cited the bank for violating ECOA after finding that the bank impermissibly used age in the pricing of certain loans. The bank was assessed a $5,000 civil money penalty.

♦ **Jefferson Bank** — The FDIC cited the bank for violating ECOA and the Fair

Housing Act after finding that the bank engaged in a pattern or practice of discrimination in 2005 and 2006 when the bank limited the choice of loan programs it offered to certain Hispanic borrowers who also qualified for other loan programs the bank offered to non-Hispanic white borrowers. The bank was assessed a $10,000 civil money penalty.

The FDIC also issued civil money penalties in 67 cases involving inaccurate HMDA data. Civil money penalties totaled approximately $400,000.

A Look Ahead

The referrals from the bank regulatory agencies and active investigations by working group members indicate that in 2011 there will be continued attention to pricing discrimination and product steering, as well as a growth in the number of matters involving redlining. In addition, the working group expects to continue to pursue its two special areas of focus from 2010: ensuring non-discrimination in loan modifications and ensuring compliance with the fair lending laws by lenders that participate in the FHA's mortgage insurance program.

Victims' Rights Committee

Introduction

The third committee created to carry out the President's Executive Order establishing the Task Force is the Victims' Rights Committee (Committee). The Committee's primary purpose is to address the needs and rights of victims of financial fraud. Accordingly, the Committee has concentrated its efforts in three areas: (1) public awareness and education through the launch of

a public website; (2) training on victims' rights and services; and (3) focusing on restitution as a priority in federal prosecutions.

The Committee is co-chaired by the Department of Justice (DOJ), Executive Office for U.S. Attorneys (EOUSA), represented by Director H. Marshall Jarrett, and the DOJ's Office of Justice Programs (OJP), represented by Principal Deputy Assistant Attorney General Mary Lou Leary. Membership in the Committee consists of many federal agencies and components, including: the Attorney General's Advisory Committee; DOJ's Criminal, Civil and Civil Rights Divisions; the FBI; the Federal Trade Commission (FTC); the U.S. Department of Housing and Urban Development (HUD); the Securities and Exchange Commission (SEC); and the U.S. Marshal's Service (USMS).

The Committee held its inaugural meeting on January 20, 2010, where the Committee co-chairs presented remarks and charged the Committee with finding ways to better meet the legal requirements and needs of victims of financial fraud. To increase the Committee's understanding of and focus on victims in such cases, the Committee asked the National Criminal Justice Reference Service to compile a comprehensive list of publications, resources and article abstracts on victimization and other issues affecting victims of financial fraud crimes. This compilation was distributed to all Committee members as well as to the Executive Director of the Task Force. Further, given that the Committee is made up of members from an incredibly diverse range of governmental entities, the Committee's initial meeting provided members with the opportunity to hear presentations from each other regarding their respective agency's programs, activities and training concerning crime victims. This exchange of information served to increase the members' understanding of the Committee's purpose as well as how each member can most effectively provide victim assistance and outreach within their particular area of responsibility.

In addition to meetings and the exchange of ideas, the Committee spent a significant portion of its energy during 2010 developing website content and training materials and considering legislative tools aimed at addressing the needs and rights of financial fraud victims. The Committee took the lead in establishing the Task Force's public website, *www.stopfraud.gov*, which was launched at DOJ's ceremony commemorating National Crime Victims' Rights Week. The website is an invaluable resource for members of the public. Specifically, the section entitled "Protect Yourself From Fraud" contains descriptions of a wide variety of financial scams and information on how best to avoid becoming a victim of financial fraud. The website is also a useful resource for all Task Force members as it contains up-to-date information on the enforcement activities of each working group.

Beyond establishing the website, the Committee has also assisted in the development of a bulletin for federal prosecutors, conducted numerous training sessions at national training events and is currently working to develop an exportable training module that can be used by investigators, prosecutors and victim service providers to improve their awareness of and response to financial fraud victims. More information about the important work of the Committee during the past year and goals for moving forward in 2011 are addressed below.

OUTREACH AND INITIATIVES

As discussed above, the Task Force's public Website, *www.stopfraud.gov*, was launched by the Attorney General as part of National Crime

Victims' Rights Week on April 16, 2010. The website was designed to be a one-stop resource for financial fraud victims and the public at large. The Committee spent considerable time compiling effective consumer resources for the first phase of the website, which were developed to provide information about how to protect individuals from financial fraud and how to report various types of financial fraud. This portion of the website is organized by type of fraud scheme, with links to appropriate existing consumer websites within each category. Additionally, the website includes links to resources from nearly all Committee member agencies, as well as other useful tools for the public. Particularly active in contributing content for the website is the FTC, which continues to provide numerous resources concerning mortgage foreclosure scams, internet scams, government grant scams, business opportunity scams, identity theft and charity fraud. *StopFraud.gov* also links to the FTC Complaint Assistant, which allows consumers to file complaints online about frauds and scams. These complaints are entered into FTC's Consumer Sentinel, a secure online database that is used by thousands of civil and criminal law enforcement authorities worldwide.

Since its launch in April 2010, the *Stop-Fraud.gov* website has received more than 1.5 million page views, with the sections concerning Mortgage Fraud, Loan and Lending Fraud, Identity Theft/Privacy Issues and Mass Marketing Fraud, Mail, Wire and Internet Fraud being visited most often. The Committee continues to add and update content to the website and has begun gathering proposed content for a new section of the site that will provide additional useful resources to consumers who have been victimized by financial fraud. The new material is expected to launch in connection with the observance of National Crime Victims' Rights Week.

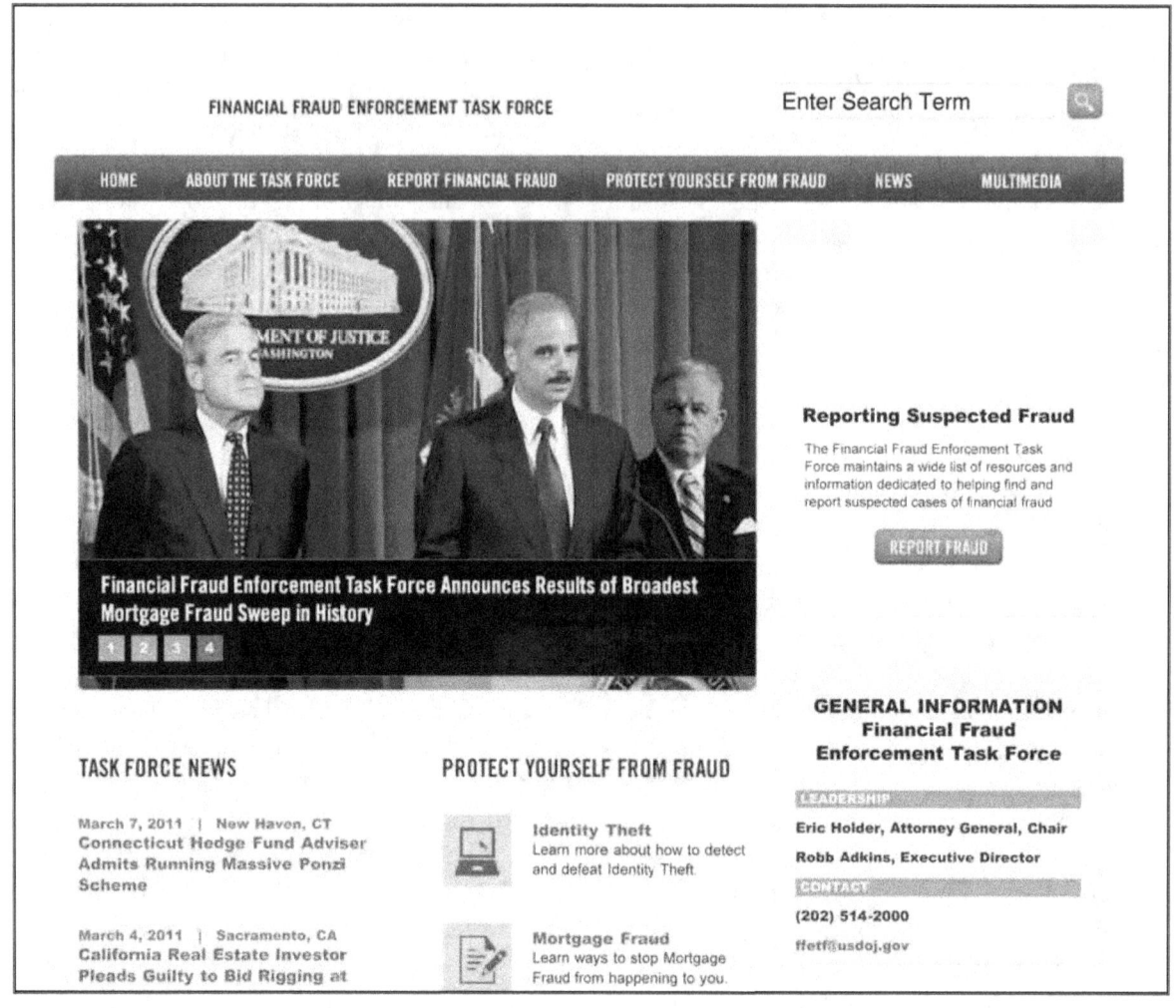

TRAINING AND COORDINATION

Members of the Committee have served as faculty at numerous training courses to educate participants about victims' rights, policy considerations and restitution in financial fraud cases. On February 25, 2010, Committee members from EOUSA and the U.S. Attorneys' Offices presented a session to Assistant U.S. Attorneys at the Asset Forfeiture Chiefs and Experts Conference at the National Advocacy Center (NAC) in Columbia, South Carolina. The session focused on using the asset forfeiture procedure to return money to victims and to satisfy restitution orders.

This presentation was repeated on May 25, 2010, at the Asset Forfeiture Support Staff Experts course. Additionally, on March 3, 2010, an EOUSA staff member taught a segment about the government's responsibility to victims at the Mortgage Fraud Task Force Conference, at the NAC, whose audience included federal, state and local prosecutors and investigators. Committee members also presented sessions on victims' rights and restitution at the U.S. Attorneys' Financial Fraud Coordinators Conference and at the Identity Theft Seminar, both held at the NAC in October 2010.

The 2010 National Center for Victims of Crime's National Conference was held in New Orleans on September 14–17, 2010. This important national conference, which included approximately 1,000 participants, provided the opportunity for several Committee members to host workshops and institutes and to make presentations to train victim advocates, prosecutors, policymakers, mental health providers and professionals about the unique needs of victims of financial fraud. The Office for Victims of Crime (OVC) served as the official conference partner for this national training event and hosted two separate workshops addressing financial fraud. The first was titled "Overview of Cyber and Financial Fraud," which addressed how financial fraud and cybercrime victims can face unique hurdles when trying to access justice, and explored the unique rights of this category of crime victims. The second was titled "Expanding Your Services To Assist and Protect Victims of Identity Theft," which showcased new tools developed by OVC and the FTC for use by victim service providers to expand their reach to victims of financial crime. At this National Conference, the Criminal Division's Asset Forfeiture and Money Laundering Section (AFMLS) staffed an exhibit booth, distributed literature and answered questions from the public, while EOUSA and the U.S. Attorney community presented at workshops relating to victims' rights and restitution in financial fraud cases.

Lastly , AFMLS conducted a two-day seminar entitled "Returning Forfeited Assets to Victims of Crime," which provided training and interface opportunities for prosecutors, agents, victim/witness professionals and other government professionals responsible for returning forfeited assets to victims. Approximately 130 government professionals attended this seminar.

In September 2010, EOUSA published an issue of USA Bulletin, an educational publication directed at the U.S. Attorney community, which concentrated on the formation and initial work of the Task Force. The issue included an article written by the Committee's co-chairs which discussed the Crime Victims' Rights Act (18 U.S.C. 3771 *et seq.*), explained the Federal Government's obligations to crime victims in the criminal justice process and highlighted the Committee's activities and goals for 2010.

In late 2010, AFMLS published *Returning Forfeited Assets to Victims of Crime: A Guide for Prosecutors, Agents, and Support Staff*. This comprehensive guide provides an overview of forfeiture as it relates to victims and step-by-step instructions for using the remission and restoration processes to return forfeited funds to victims. Further, AFMLS introduced a section devoted solely to victim issues on its internal website, *AFML Online*. This section provides government professionals and investigators with relevant information pertaining to the remission and restoration of forfeited assets to victims. The information includes AFMLS publications, such as the new *Returning Forfeited Assets to Victims of Crime* guide, regulations and policies, sample requests, forms and case summaries.

Collaboration With Other Task Force Members

In an effort to further expand its role in training, the Victims' Rights Committee briefed and provided a training module sample to the Training and Information Sharing Committee regarding the use and value of exportable training modules for law enforcement and prosecutor-based trainings on financial fraud victims' issues. The training components included information on victim impact, victims' rights, victim restitution, asset recovery, and forfeiture and victim resources. As a result of the briefing, a representative from the Federal Law Enforcement Training Center (FLETC) Financial Fraud Institute expressed interest in having the Committee work to develop generic victim training modules that could be added to their Introduction to Fraud Investigation Training Program.

In mid-2010, the Deputy Attorney General convened a Victims of Crime Working Group and tasked it with revising the *Attorney General Guidelines for Victim and Witness Assistance* (Guidelines), which were last updated in 2005. The Committee worked with the Victims of Crime Working Group to draft language for the financial fraud and identity theft sections of the new Guidelines, which are expected to be implemented by mid 2011.

Legislative Efforts

Mindful that the President's Executive Order explains that one of the purposes of the Task Force is to "recover the proceeds of such crimes and violations, and ensure just and effective punishment," the Committee devoted significant time to examining impediments to the collection of full and timely restitution for victims of crime. The Committee continues to explore the role of potential legislative solutions to improve the efficiency and effectiveness of services and restitution for victims. The Committee will continue to work with the Department of Justice's Office of Legislative Affairs to identify any potential legislative solutions.

SIGNIFICANT ACCOMPLISHMENTS

The following is a summary of some of the significant actions and accomplishments of the members of the Victims' Rights Committee:

Office of Justice Programs/Office for Victims of Crime

The OJP within DOJ has a unique role to play in helping to prevent financial fraud, including identity theft, and in assisting victims. In addition, OJP strives to ensure that local law enforcement and victims' advocates receive training regarding proper responses to the large number of individuals who fall prey to financial fraud. OVC announced a Financial and Non-Violent Crimes Fellowship to assess the needs and rights of vulnerable victims of financial fraud and other forms of serious yet nonviolent crime (identity theft, medical/pharmaceutical fraud, mortgage fraud, computer intrusions, international cyber crimes, etc.). The Fellowship offers OVC a more comprehensive victim assistance strategy that addresses gaps in traditional victim services and develops model practice recommendations for this large, yet underserved, victim population. OVC also launched a new electronic publication, *Expanding Services To Reach Victims of Identity Theft and Financial Fraud,* which summarizes the efforts of four grantees to expand their services to assist victims at the local, state, regional and national levels. This electronic publication includes practical tools to set up program infrastructure and training for staff, pro bono attorneys, law enforcement and other professionals; to equip victims with the necessary information to help themselves; and to stage an effective public outreach— all without a major outlay of financial or human resources.

U.S. Attorneys' Offices and Asset Forfeiture and Money Laundering Section — Recovery and Return of Funds to Victims

During the first year of the Task Force, the U.S. Attorneys' Offices (USAOs) collected more than $690,000,000 in criminal restitution and fines in financial fraud cases. While restitution goes directly to the victims, criminal fines are deposited into the Crime Victims Fund which is used to provide monies for victim compensation programs, victim-related training and victim assistance programs around the country. In Fiscal Year 2010, AFMLS authorized the return of more than $215 million in forfeited proceeds to victims of financial fraud in cases prosecuted by the USAOs and AFMLS. Further, in the first half of Fiscal Year 2011, more than $160 million was authorized for return to victims. Recent significant recoveries include:

- **United States v. $40,269,890.20, et al. ("World Ocean Farm")**

Isamu Kuroiwa, a citizen of Japan, claimed to operate highly profitable shrimp farms in the Philippines that generated 100 percent annual return on investment. In reality, the farms were a small fraction of the size advertised, never turned a profit and never exported any shrimp. More than 10,000 investors suffered cumulative losses of at least $230 million. Kuroiwa pleaded guilty to fraud charges. The FBI seized funds that Kuroiwa attempted to launder in the United States, and AFMLS brought an in rem forfeiture action against the funds. On March 12, 2010, the court entered a default order of forfeiture of $40 million. On January 28, 2011, AFMLS authorized remission of the forfeited funds to the Japanese bankruptcy administrator for distribution to the victims.

- **United States v. Hassan Nemazee**

Between 1997 and 2009, Hassan Nemazee used false documentation to obtain multiple lines of credit worth hundreds of millions of dollars from various banks. Nemazee was prosecuted by the U.S. Attorney's Office for the Southern District of New York and was convicted of wire and bank fraud and ordered to pay more than $292 million in restitution to three victim financial institutions. Various assets valued at approximately $78 million were forfeited as proceeds of the scheme. On November 19, 2010, AFMLS approved restoration of the forfeited proceeds to the three victims.

- **United States v. Marc Dreier**

Marc Dreier sold fraudulent promissory notes to multiple hedge funds, investment funds and pension funds. The U.S. Attorney's Office for the Southern District of New York successfully prosecuted Dreier, and on July 15, 2009, Dreier was convicted of conspiracy, wire fraud, money laundering and securities fraud and ordered to pay more than $389 million in restitution to 26 victims. On August 31, 2010, the court ordered the forfeiture of various assets valued at approximately $80 million, which will be returned to victims through the restoration process.

- **United States v. Richard Alyn Waage ("Tri-West Investment Club")**

On October 14, 2010, AFMLS released remission payments totaling $8 million to 4,965 victims of the Tri-West Investment Club Ponzi scheme. Canadian Alyn Richard Waage and co-conspirators induced thousands of victims to invest by falsely representing, through the Internet and other media, that the investments would earn 10 percent or more per month through a special bank debenture trading program. Inevitably, the scheme collapsed and investors lost more than $30 million. The Internal Revenue Service and the FBI seized foreign bank accounts and real properties in Mexico and Costa Rica, a yacht, a helicopter, numerous late-model vehicles and jewelry. The U.S. Attorney's Office for the Eastern District of California successfully prosecuted Waage and his co-conspirators on various fraud charges and obtained forfeiture of the assets. In September 2010, AFMLS authorized disbursement of the forfeited funds to the victims.

Federal Trade Commission

The FTC pairs every law enforcement action with relevant consumer education. Web pages, videos, flyers, audio messages and other resources for consumers, businesses and media are posted to maximize education about cases. For example, a video, *Don't Pay for a Promise*, offers information for job hunters about recognizing and avoiding job placement scams. Another, *Dealing with Debt Collectors*, explains the rights of people in debt, the responsibilities of legitimate debt collectors and several illegal debt collection schemes. *10 Things You Can Do to Avoid Fraud*, a brochure, is a practical tip sheet to avoiding common frauds and scams.

A LOOK AHEAD

Looking ahead, the Committee will continue to pursue goals relating to training. First, the Committee will work with FLETC to develop modules for its Introduction to Fraud Training program. The Committee also intends to continue developing strategies to increase the cooperation among asset forfeiture units, financial litigation units, and criminal prosecutors at the U.S. Attorneys' Offices. This will be accomplished through collaborative training of both prosecutors and law enforcement agents. As always, the Committee will seek to identify and address any emerging areas where the needs and rights of victims of financial fraud require increased attention.

Appendix A.
Executive Order

Appendix A

THE WHITE HOUSE

Office of the Press Secretary

For Immediate Release   November 17, 2009

EXECUTIVE ORDER

- - - - - - -

ESTABLISHMENT OF THE FINANCIAL FRAUD ENFORCEMENT TASK FORCE

By the authority vested in me as President by the Constitution and the laws of the United States of America, and in order to strengthen the efforts of the Department of Justice, in conjunction with Federal, State, tribal, territorial, and local agencies, to investigate and prosecute significant financial crimes and other violations relating to the current financial crisis and economic recovery efforts, recover the proceeds of such crimes and violations, and ensure just and effective punishment of those who perpetrate financial crimes and violations, it is hereby ordered as follows:

Section 1. Establishment. There is hereby established an interagency Financial Fraud Enforcement Task Force (Task Force) led by the Department of Justice.

Sec. 2. Membership and Operation. The Task Force shall be chaired by the Attorney General and consist of senior-level officials from the following departments, agencies, and offices, selected by the heads of the respective departments, agencies, and offices in consultation with the Attorney General:

(a)   the Department of Justice;
(b)   the Department of the Treasury;
(c)   the Department of Commerce;
(d)   the Department of Labor;
(e)   the Department of Housing and Urban Development;
(f)   the Department of Education;
(g)   the Department of Homeland Security;
(h)   the Securities and Exchange Commission;
(i)   the Commodity Futures Trading Commission;
(j)   the Federal Trade Commission;
(k)   the Federal Deposit Insurance Corporation;
(l)   the Board of Governors of the Federal Reserve System;
(m)   the Federal Housing Finance Agency;

more

2

(n)   the Office of Thrift Supervision;

(o)   the Office of the Comptroller of the Currency;

(p)   the Small Business Administration;

(q)   the Federal Bureau of Investigation;

(r)   the Social Security Administration;

(s)   the Internal Revenue Service, Criminal Investigations;

(t)   the Financial Crimes Enforcement Network;

(u)   the United States Postal Inspection Service;

(v)   the United States Secret Service;

(w)   the United States Immigration and Customs Enforcement;

(x)   relevant Offices of Inspectors General and related Federal entities, including without limitation the Office of the Inspector General for the Department of Housing and Urban Development, the Recovery Accountability and Transparency Board, and the Office of the Special Inspector General for the Troubled Asset Relief Program; and

(y)   such other executive branch departments, agencies, or offices as the President may, from time to time, designate or that the Attorney General may invite.

The Attorney General shall convene and, through the Deputy Attorney General, direct the work of the Task Force in fulfilling all its functions under this order. The Attorney General shall convene the first meeting of the Task Force within 30 days of the date of this order and shall thereafter convene the Task Force at such times as he deems appropriate. At the direction of the Attorney General, the Task Force may establish subgroups consisting exclusively of Task Force members or their designees under this section, including but not limited to a Steering Committee chaired by the Deputy Attorney General, and subcommittees addressing enforcement efforts, training and information sharing, and victims' rights, as the Attorney General deems appropriate.

Sec. 3. Mission and Functions. Consistent with the authorities assigned to the Attorney General by law, and other applicable law, the Task Force shall:

(a)   provide advice to the Attorney General for the investigation and prosecution of cases of bank, mortgage, loan, and lending fraud; securities and commodities fraud; retirement plan fraud; mail and wire fraud; tax crimes; money laundering; False Claims Act violations; unfair competition; discrimination; and other financial crimes and violations (hereinafter financial crimes and violations), when such cases are determined by the Attorney General, for purposes of this order, to be significant;

3

(b)   make recommendations to the Attorney General, from
      time to time, for action to enhance cooperation among
      Federal, State, local, tribal, and territorial
      authorities responsible for the investigation and
      prosecution of significant financial crimes and
      violations; and

(c)   coordinate law enforcement operations with
      representatives of State, local, tribal, and
      territorial law enforcement.

Sec. 4. Coordination with State, Local, Tribal, and
Territorial Law Enforcement. Consistent with the objectives
set out in this order, and to the extent permitted by law,
the Attorney General is encouraged to invite the following
representatives of State, local, tribal, and territorial law
enforcement to participate in the Task Force's subcommittee
addressing enforcement efforts in the subcommittee's performance
of the functions set forth in section 3(c) of this order
relating to the coordination of Federal, State, local, tribal,
and territorial law enforcement operations involving financial
crimes and violations:

(a)   the National Association of Attorneys General;

(b)   the National District Attorneys Association; and

(c)   such other representatives of State, local, tribal,
      and territorial law enforcement as the Attorney
      General deems appropriate.

Sec. 5. Outreach. Consistent with the law enforcement
objectives set out in this order, the Task Force, in accordance
with applicable law, in addition to regular meetings, shall
conduct outreach with representatives of financial institutions,
corporate entities, nonprofit organizations, State, local,
tribal, and territorial governments and agencies, and other
interested persons to foster greater coordination and
participation in the detection and prosecution of financial
fraud and financial crimes, and in the enforcement of antitrust
and antidiscrimination laws.

Sec. 6. Administration. The Department of Justice, to
the extent permitted by law and subject to the availability of
appropriations, shall provide administrative support and funding
for the Task Force.

Sec. 7. General Provisions. (a) Nothing in this order
shall be construed to impair or otherwise affect:

(i)   authority granted by law to an executive
       department, agency, or the head thereof, or the
       status of that department or agency within the
       Federal Government; or

(ii)   functions of the Director of the Office of
       Management and Budget relating to budgetary,
       administrative, or legislative proposals.

more

4

(b) This Task Force shall replace, and continue the
     work of, the Corporate Fraud Task Force created by
     Executive Order 13271 of July 9, 2002. Executive
     Order 13271 is hereby terminated pursuant to section 6
     of that order.

(c) This order shall be implemented consistent with
     applicable law and subject to the availability of
     appropriations.

(d) This order is not intended to, and does not, create
     any right or benefit, substantive or procedural,
     enforceable at law or in equity by any party against
     the United States, its departments, agencies, or
     entities, its officers, employees, or agents, or any
     other person.

Sec. 8. Termination. The Task Force shall terminate
when directed by the President or, with the approval of the
President, by the Attorney General.

                    BARACK OBAMA

THE WHITE HOUSE,
     November 17, 2009.

                         ###

Appendix B.
Financial Fraud Coordinators' Directory

Appendix B

FINANCIAL FRAUD COORDINATORS' DIRECTORY

District/Division   *Name/Address*

Office of Deputy Attorney General......................Adkins, Robb, Executive Director
Financial Fraud Enforcement Task Force
Department of Justice
950 Pennsylvania Ave., NW
Washington, DC 20530

Executive Office for U.S. Attorneys.....................Varnado, Jason, AUSA
Smith, Judy, AUSA
600 E Street, NW
BICN. Bldg., Room 7600
Washington, DC 20530

Criminal Division, DOJ.......................................Lurie, Adam, Senior Counsel to the AAG
Suleiman, Daniel, Counsel to the AAG
Department of Justice
950 Pennsylvania Ave., NW
Washington, DC 20530

Civil Division, DOJ..Graber, Geoffrey, Office of the AAG
Department of Justice
950 Pennsylvania Ave., NW
Washington, DC 20530

Civil Rights Division, DOJ..................................Halperin, Eric, Special Counsel to the AAG
Department of Justice
950 Pennsylvania Ave., NW
Washington, DC 20530

Antiturst Division, DOJ......................................Terzaken, John, Assistant Chief
Department of Justice
950 Pennsylvania Ave., NW
Washington, DC 20530

Middle District of Alabama................................Schiff, Andrew, AUSA
Acting Chief, Criminal Division
United States Attorney's Office
131 Clayton Street
Montgomery, Alabama 36101

Northern District of Alabama..............................Posey, Robert, AUSA
United States Attorney's Office
1801 Fourth Avenue North
Birmingham, Alabama 35203

Southern District of Alabama............................Bordenkircher, Greg AUSA
United States Attorney's Office
Riverview Plaza, 63 S. Royal St.
Suite 600
Mobile, Alabama 36602

District of Alaska.. Feldis, Kevin, AUSA
United States Attorney's Office
222 West Seventh Avenue, #9, Room 253
Anchorage, Alaska 99513-7567

District of Arizona...Lopez, John, AUSA
United States Attorney's Office
Two Renaissance Square
40 North Central, Suite 1200
Phoenix, Arizona 85004-4408

Eastern District of Arkansas...............................Vena, George, AUSA
United States Attorney's Office
425 W. Capitol, 5th Floor, Ste 500
Little Rock, Arkansas 72201

Western District of Arkansas.............................. Plumlee, Christopher D., AUSA
United States Attorney's Office
414 Parker Avenue
Fort Smith, Arkansas 72901

Central District of California..............................Kim, Beong-Soo, AUSA
United States Attorney's Office
312 N. Spring St., 17th Floor
Los Angeles, California 90012

Eastern District of California..............................Rimon, Laurel, AUSA
Chief, Special Prosecutions Unit
United States Attorney's Office
501 I Street, Room 10-100
Sacramento, California 95814

Eastern District of California, *cont.* .... Boone, Stanley, AUSA
Chief, White Collar Crime Unit
United States Attorney's Office
2500 Tulare St., Room 4401
Fresno, CA 93720

Northern District of California............................Sprague, Doug, AUSA
Adam Reeves, AUSA
United States Attorney's Office
450 Golden Gate Avenue
Box 36055
San Francisco, California 94102

Southern District of California............................Beste, Eric, AUSA
United States Attorney's Office
880 Front Street, Room 6293
San Diego, California 92101

District of Colorado..Kirsch, Matthew, AUSA
Chief, Economic Crimes Section
United States Attorney's Office
Suite 1200, Federal Office Building
1225 17th Street, Suite 700
Denver, Colorado 80202

District of Columbia..Connor, Deborah, AUSA
Chief, Fraud and Public Corruption Section
United States Attorney's Office
Judiciary Center Building
555 4th Street, NW, Room 5253
Washington, D.C. 20530

District of Connecticut...Glover, Eric, AUSA
United States Attorney's Office
Connecticut Financial Center
157 Church Street, 23rd Floor
New Haven, Connecticut 06510

District of Delaware..Burke, Christopher, AUSA
United States Attorney's Office
Nemours Building
P.O. Box 2046
Wilmington, Delaware 19899

Middle District of Florida.....................................O'Neill, Robert, AUSA
United States Attorney's Office
400 North Tampa Street, Suite 3200
Tampa, Florida 33602

Northern District of Florida............................... Kunz, Stephen M., Supervisory AUSA
United States Attorney's Office
111 North Adams Street, 4th Fl
Tallahassee, Florida 32301

Southern District of Florida................................Silverstein, Joan, AUSA
United States Attorney's Office
Federal Justice Building
99 NE Fourth Street
Miami, Florida 33132

Middle District of Georgia...................................McCommon, Paul C., III, AUSA
United States Attorney's Office
Thomas Jefferson Building
300 Mulberry Street, 4th Floor
Macon, Georgia 31201

Northern District of Georgia............................... Chartash, Randy, AUSA
United States Attorney's Office
Richard Russell Building, Suite 600
75 Spring Street, SW
Atlanta, Georgia 30303

Southern District of Georgia...............................Durham, James D., First Assistant USA
United States Attorney's Office
100 Bull Street, Suite 201
Savannah, Georgia 31412

District of Guam...David, Marivic P., AUSA
United States Attorney's Office
Sirena Plaza
108 Hernan Cortez, Suite 500
Hagatna, Guam 96910

District of Hawaii...Osborne, Jr., Leslie E., AUSA
United States Attorney's Office
300 Ala Moana Blvd., Room 6-100
Honolulu, Hawaii 96850

District of Idaho..Breitsameter, George W., AUSA
United States Attorney's Office
800 Park Blvd., Suite 600
Boise, ID 83712

Central District of Illinois.....................................Knauss, Darilynn, AUSA, Branch Chief
United States Attorney's Office
One Technology Plaza
211 Fulton Street, Ste 400
Peoria, Illinois 61602

Northern District of Illinois................................Conway, James M., AUSA
Chief, Financial Crimes & Special Prosec.
United States Attorney's Office
Everett McKinley Dirksen Building
Chicago, Illinois 60604

Southern District of Illinois.................................Smith, Norman R., AUSA
United States Attorney's Office
Nine Executive Drive, Suite 300
Fairview Heights, Illinois 62208

Northern District of Indiana................................Houston, Toi Denise, AUSA
United States Attorney's Office
5400 Federal Plaza, Suite 1500
Hammond, Indiana 46320

Southern District of Indiana................................McKee, Christina, Criminal Chief
United States Attorney's Office
10 West Market Street, Suite 2100
Indianapolis, Indiana 46204-3048

Northern District of Iowa....................................Berry, Sean, AUSA
United States Attorney's Office
Hach Building
401 1st Street, SE, Suite 401
Cedar Rapids, Iowa 52401-1825

Southern District of Iowa....................................Kahl, Andrew H., AUSA
United States Attorney's Office
110 East Court Avenue, Room 286
Des Moines, Iowa 50309

District of Kansas...Hathaway, Rich, AUSA
United States Attorney's Office
444 SE Quincy Street, Ste 290
Topeka, Kansas 66683

Eastern District of Kentucky..............................Catron, Frances, AUSA
United States Attorney's Office
260 W. Vine Street, #300
Lexington, Kentucky 40507

Western District of Kentucky..............................Ford, Marisa J., AUSA
United States Attorney's Office
Bank of Louisville Building
510 West Broadway, 10th Floor
Louisville, Kentucky 40202

Eastern District of Louisiana.............................. Mann, James, AUSA
United States Attorney's Office
Hale Boggs Federal Building
500 Poydras Street, Room B-210
New Orleans, Louisiana 70130

Middle District of Louisiana...............................Amundson, Corey, AUSA
Deputy Criminal Chief
United States Attorney's Office
Russell B. Long Federal Building
777 Florida Street, Suite 208
Baton Rouge, Louisiana 70801

Western District of Louisiana..............................Jarzabek, Joseph G., AUSA
United States Attorney's Office
300 Fannin Street, Suite 3201
Shreveport, Louisiana 71101-3068

District of Maine...Chapman, Jonathan R., AUSA
United States Attorney's Office
100 Middle Street
East Tower, 6th Floor
Portland, Maine 04101

District of Maryland...Su, Jonathan C., AUSA
United States Attorney's Office
6500 Cherrywood Lane
Suite 400
Greenbelt, Maryland 20770

District of Massachusetts......................................Walters, Sarah E., AUSA
United States Attorney's Office
United States Courthouse
1 Courthouse Way, Suite 9200
Boston, Massachusetts 02210

Eastern District of Michigan...............................Reynolds, Karen, AUSA
United States Attorney's Office
211 W. Fort Street, Suite 2001
Detroit, Michigan 48226

Western District of Michigan..............................Delaney, Brian K., AUSA
United States Attorney's Office
330 Ionia, NW, 5th Floor
Grand Rapids, Michigan 49503-0208
(616) 456-2404
Brian.Delaney@usdoj.gov

District of Minnesota...Dixon, Joe, AUSA
United States Attorney's Office
300 S. 4th Street, Suite 600
Minneapolis, Minnesota 55415

Northern District of Mississippi..........................Mims, Robert J., AUSA
United States Attorney's Office
900 Jefferson Avenue
Oxford, Mississippi 38655

Southern District of Mississippi.......................... Hurst, Mike, AUSA
United States Attorney's Office
188 East Capitol St., Suite 500
Jackson, Mississippi 39201

Eastern District of Missouri...............................Muchnick, Steven A.
United States Attorney's Office
111 S. 10th Street, Room 20.333
St. Louis, Missouri 63102

Western District of Missouri...............................Mahoney, Kate, AUSA
United States Attorney's Office
Charles Evans Whittaker Courthouse
400 E. Ninth Street, 5th Floor
Kansas City, Missouri 64106

District of Montana.. Archer, Ryan M., AUSA
United States Attorney's Office
Western Security Bank Bldg
2929 3rd Avenue, North, Ste 400
Billings, Montana 59101

District of Nebraska... Everett, Alan L., AUSA
United States Attorney's Office
487 Federal Bldg., 100 Centennial Mall North
Lincoln, Nebraska 68508

District of Nevada.. Vasquez, Timothy S., AUSA
United States Attorney's Office
333 South Las Vegas Blvd., Suite 5000
Las Vegas, Nevada 89101

District of New Hampshire................................. Kinsella, Robert M., AUSA
United States Attorney's Office
53 Pleasant Street, 4th Floor
Concord, New Hampshire 03301

District of New Jersey... Germano, Judith, AUSA
Chief, Economic Crimes Unit
United States Attorney's Office
970 Broad Street, Suite 700
Newark, New Jersey 07102

District of New Mexico....................................... Higgins, Mary, AUSA
United States Attorney's Office
201 Third Street, NW, Suite 900
Albuquerque, New Mexico 87102

Eastern District of New York............................... McMahon, James (Jay), AUSA
Chief, Bus. & Secur. Fraud Section
United States Attorney's Office
271 Cadman Plaza East
Brooklyn, New York 11201

Northern District of New York............................ Storch, Robert P., AUSA
Counsel to U.S. Attorney
United States Attorney's Office
James Foley Federal Bldg.
445 Broadway, Room 218
Albany, NY 12207-2924

Southern District of New York..............................Jonas, Bonnie, AUSA
United States Attorney's Office
One St. Andrews Plaza
New York, New York 10007

Western District of New York..............................Resnick, Richard, AUSA
United States Attorney's Office
620 Federal Bldg., 100 State Street
Rochester, New York 12207

Eastern District of North Carolina.......................Wheeler, Clay, AUSA
United States Attorney's Office
Suite 800, Federal Building
310 New Bern Avenue
Raleigh, North Carolina 27601-1461

Middle District of North Carolina.......................Chut, Frank, AUSA
United States Attorney's Office
101 S. Edgeworth St.
4th Floor
Greensboro, North Carolina 27401

Western District of North Carolina......................Meyers, Kurt, AUSA
United States Attorney's Office
227 West Trade Street, Suite 1650
Charlotte, North Carolina 28202

District of North Dakota.....................................Jordheim, Lynn C., AUSA
United States Attorney's Office
655 First Avenue, North
Ste 250
Fargo, North Dakota 58102

Northern District of Ohio...................................Rowland, Ann C.,
Chief, Major Frauds and Corruption
United States Attorney's Office
801 West Superior Avenue
Suite 400
Cleveland, Ohio 44113

Southern District of Ohio...................................Shoemaker, Brenda, AUSA
Chief, Financial Crimes
United States Attorney's Office
303 Marconi Boulevard
Suite 200
Columbus, Ohio 43215

Eastern District of Oklahoma..............................**Guthrie, Gay, AUSA**
United States Attorney's Office
1200 West Okmulgee Street
Muskogee, Oklahoma 74401

Northern District of Oklahoma...........................**Gallant, Jeff, AUSA**
United States Attorney's Office
110 West 7th Street
Suite 300
Tulsa, Oklahoma 74119-1029

Western District of Oklahoma ....**Kelly, Kerry A., AUSA**
United States Attorney's Office
210 West Park Avenue, Suite 400
Oklahoma City, Oklahoma 73102

District of Oregon...**Caldwell, Lance, AUSA**
United States Attorney's Office
Mark O. Hatfield U.S. Courthouse
1000 SW Third Avenue, Suite 600
Portland, Oregon 97204-2902

Eastern District of Pennsylvania..........................**Goldberg, Richard, AUSA**
Chief, Financial Institution Fraud Unit
United States Attorney's Office
615 Chestnut Street, Suite 1250
Philadelphia, Pennsylvania 19106-4476

Middle District of Pennsylvania...........................**Brandler, Bruce, AUSA**
United States Attorney's Office
Suite 220, Federal Building
228 Walnut Street
Harrisburg, Pennsylvania 17108

Western District of Pennsylvania.........................**Cessar, Robert, AUSA**
United States Attorney's Office
633 USPO & Courthouse, Suite 4000
7th Avenue & 700 Grant Street
Pittsburgh, Pennsylvania 15219

District of Puerto Rico..**Lopez, Ernesto, AUSA**
United States Attorney's Office
Torre Chardon, Suite 1201
350 Carlos Chardon Avenue
San Juan, Puerto Rico 00918

District of Rhode Island... Reich, Andrew J., AUSA
United States Attorney's Office
Fleet Center
50 Kennedy Plaza, 8th Floor
Providence, Rhode Island 02903

District of South Carolina.................................... Watkins, William, AUSA
United States Attorney's Office
First Union Bldg.
105 Spring Street, Suite 200
Greenville, South Carolina 29063

District of South Dakota..................................... Zuercher, David, AUSA
United States Attorney's Office
225 South Pierre Street, Room 337
Pierre, South Dakota 57501-2489

Eastern District of Tennessee.............................. Cook, Steve H., AUSA
Chief, Criminal Division
United States Attorney's Office
800 Market Street, Suite 211
Knoxville, Tennessee 37902

Middle District of Tennessee.............................. Webb, John, Branch Chief
United States Attorney's Office
110 9th Avenue South, Suite A-961
Nashville, Tennessee 37203

Western District of Tennessee............................ André, Carroll, AUSA
United States Attorney's Office
800 Clifford Davis Federal Office Bldg.
167 North Main Street
Memphis, Tennessee 38103

Eastern District of Texas...................................... Shipchandler, Shamoil, AUSA
Deputy Criminal Chief
United States Attorney's Office
101 East Park Blvd., Ste 500
Plano, Texas 75074

Northern District of Texas................................... Saldana, Sarah, AUSA
United States Attorney's Office
1100 Commerce Street, Ste 300
Dallas, Texas 75242

Southern District of Texas....................................Buchanan, James (Jim) R.,
Deputy Criminal Chief
United States Attorney's Office
919 Milam Street, Suite 1500
P.O. Box 61129
Houston, Texas 77208-1129

Western District of Texas....................................Lane, Mark, AUSA
United States Attorney's Office
816 Congress Ave., Ste 1000
Austin, Texas 78701

District of Utah...Washburn, Loren, AUSA
United States Attorney's Office
185 South State, Suite 400
Salt Lake City, Utah 84111

District of Vermont..Waples, Gregory, AUSA
United States Attorney's Office
Federal Building
11 Elmwood Avenue, 3rd Floor
Burlington, Vermont 05401

District of the Virgin Islands...............................Chisholm, Kim, AUSA
United States Attorney's Office
Federal Building & Crthse
5500 Veterans Drive, Room 260
St. Thomas, Virgin Islands 00802

Eastern District of Virginia.................................Dry, Michael, AUSA
United States Attorney's Office
600 E. Main St, Ste 1800
Richmond, Virginia 23219

Western District of Virginia................................Hogeboom, III, C. Patrick, AUSA
United States Attorney's Office
310 1st Street, SW
Roanoke, Virginia 24011

Eastern District of Washington...........................Harrington, Joseph H., Criminal Chief
United States Attorney's Office
920 W. Riverside, Suite 340
Spokane, Washington 99210

Western District of Washington............................ Blackstone, Carl, AUSA
United States Attorney's Office
700 Stewart Street, Suite 5220
Seattle, Washington 98101-1271

Northern District of West Virginia........................Stein, Michael, AUSA
United States Attorney's Office
1125 Chapline Street, Ste 3000
Wheeling, West Virginia 26003

Southern District of West Virginia........................Robinson, Susan M., AUSA
United States Attorney's Office
300 Virginia Street, East, Room 4000
Charleston, West Virginia 25301

Eastern District of Wisconsin.............................. Haanstad, Gregory, AUSA
Deputy Criminal Chief
United States Attorney's Office
517 East Wisconsin Avenue
Milwaukee, Wisconsin 53202

Western District of Wisconsin............................. Vaudreuil, John W., United States Attorney
United States Attorney's Office
660 West Washington Avenue, Suite 303
Madison, Wisconsin 53703

District of Wyoming...Leschuck, Lisa E., AUSA
United States Attorney's Office
2120 Capitol Avenue, Room 4002
Cheyenne, Wyoming 82001

www.ingramcontent.com/pod-product-compliance
Lightning Source LLC
Chambersburg PA
CBHW081328310526
45789CB00018B/2499